The Right Kind of Loud

Finding Your Communication Voice

Kim A. Page

Lakeside Press
NEW YORK

Cover design by ArtHaus Visual Communications Ltd.
Photography by Lisbeth Hjort

ISBN: 1982073845
ISBN 13: 978-1982073848
Lakeside Press, New York, NY

PRAISE FOR

The Right Kind of Loud

"This book does more than just teach you critical skills. As you're reading, you can feel Kim's presence taking you on her journey and sharing with you the lessons she's learned, ending up as powerful communication tools."

— *Jaffar Mahmoud, Creative Content Writer, Expo 2020*

"Kim shares her incredible depth of experience, with pearls of wisdom and empathic encouragement for the reader. She surely has a sixth (and possibly seventh!) sense for helping us all achieve more authentic, empowered communication."

— *Jeff Crerie, PhD, Visual Designer and Producer, Kaiam*

"The author has a unique writing style that is witty, smart, and often whimsical, keeping you continually engaged. It gave me key takeaways that have opened my eyes to my communication style, and I will continue on this self-discovery moving forward."

— *Debbie Dowling, Learning and Development Specialist, Emirates Leisure Retail*

"*The Right Kind of Loud* is as much a professional guide about communication as a soul opener. This book makes communication human and gives the readers the confidence to integrate their own personality in their communication style rather than imposing recipes onto themselves."

— *Laura Toma, Entrepreneur and Education Consultant*

"*The Right Kind of Loud* opened up a new way for me to look at the voice and the art of the performance in presenting. I highly recommend this book to people who are seeking their own voice in today's noisy world."

— *Mato Horniacek, Co-Founder and CEO, Everest Notes*

"*The Right Kind of Loud* quickly gets to the essence of how to be heard using a rich array of simple-to-understand communication exercises and supportive anecdotes."

— *Steve Hamilton-Clark, Executive and Leadership Performance Coach*

"The main quality that stands out for me about this author is her genuineness. She has lived every word."

— *Disha Jana, Country Head of HR, Panalpina*

"I couldn't put the book down and wanted to read more. Truly informative and mind engaging. A must read for anyone who wants to become the best version of him or herself."

— *Hayat Faysal, Yoga Instructor and Holistic Healer*

To my participants and clients, with gratitude

CONTENTS

Foreword

I came to know Kim in my role as director of talent management at DP World. We needed someone to develop communication skills with our executive team members, and Kim facilitated several intimate coaching groups for us. The effects of these sessions were tangible to everyone I talked to as part of preparing this foreword. They described how Kim created a safe and inspiring environment, enabling them to make a lasting impact on their audiences. And there was a quality in her sessions that is unusual. Kim is an exceptional listener, allowing her to tailor the sessions to the needs of her participants.

I was happy to hear that Kim decided to share her knowledge and write a book. This way her experience and toolbox will be available for more of us. *The Right Kind of Loud* helps us deal with people, negotiating and resolving conflicts. This book makes it easy and accessible to find our communication mastery, and I love how she uses examples from her own life, both professional and personal, giving the theories realness and heart.

Reading the book, I had new insights, making me reflect on my own behavior in a different light. The day to day of an executive has many challenges, and we are constantly struggling with limited amount of time on our hands. We need to get things done fast, and at the same time, we are pulled into a multitude of different topics that are going on around us. A scheduled thirty-minute meeting often becomes five minutes, and during that short moment, we need to be sure that our message is received and understood, as we only have that one chance.

In a moment like this, making sure our voice has the right tone can make all the difference. The first chapter is dedicated to the voice. Indeed, each chapter of the book offers best practices to be applied in high-stake encounters. *The Right Kind of Loud* helps us reach each other and hear each other and, ultimately, do what it is that we wish to do as team members and business leaders. More than that, it helps us become the best version of our self.

Hope you will enjoy the book just like I did.

Latifa Mohammad
Dubai, UAE

Introduction
How to Read This Book

A couple of the test readers of my manuscript asked me to add something about my professional profile in the introduction. We want to know who the author is, why should we listen to her? Having grown up in a Nordic culture, where self promotion is a sin, my instinctual answer was, well, the whole book has my personal imprint, so why would I add more accomplishments in the first part? After some reflecting and looking in other books, I gave in, realizing it's a good way to start, simply rolling it out. Here we go.

Since the beginning of my career, I have designed and delivered hundreds of workshops, talks, and individual coaching sessions. Having lived and worked in three continents and nine countries, I am fluent and able to deliver in six languages. I've had thousands of participants in my hands, and it's hard to think of a profession I haven't supported. Lawyers, politicians, scientists, financial directors, managing partners, programmers, business owners, civil engineers—the list goes on. All the while I've been transitioning from one home base to the next, entering new markets as well as cultural codes to navigate by. The methods in this book have been tested and used by countless clients in different contexts and countries, and they are the pillars of my own career journey. Starting out as an artist, I became a trainer when the thrill of expressing myself was widened into the satisfaction of helping others express themselves. When I transitioned into the corporate world, the focus became helping my clients use the skills we were working on to achieve their professional goals. My expertise grew into the area of interpersonal communication—the things we do when we interact with each other.

We often think of communication as a way to get our message through. And sure, it is. But it is more than that. Sometimes the right thing is to wait, finding the right moment. Sometimes silence can be the most effective tool. Other times we need to raise our voice. Getting The Right Kind of Loud means knowing how to adjust to the person you are trying to reach, fine-tuning to the situation and the kind of influence you are looking for. To get there, we need to bring our whole self along together with our listening capacity. Connection is created when we feel that the other person is real, willing to share from his or her experiences. Using the now as a starting point, it helps to be rooted in the moment, drawing on embodiment and grounded presence. And if you can let go of agendas and expectations and be responsive when you interact with others, whatever needs to happen will unfold easier and faster than with a rigid approach.

This book is written to help you expand your comfort zone, connecting with the people in the room, on stage, in meetings and boardrooms, in interviews, and during sales pitches. The goal is for you to be the Right Kind of Loud, engaging in any kind of situation you walk into. It's a collection of reflections, methods, and exercises gathered from my years as a trainer in the communication field. The book is arranged into seven chapters of learning areas for you to choose from like a menu. You'll notice that the chapters are interrelated, and you can start wherever your curiosity takes you or read from A to Z. If you would like to go straight to the hands-on exercises in the book, there's an appendix on page 129 with an overview, and for those of you puzzled by some of the expressions in use, I've added a glossary on page 131 with clarifications. The last chapter offers a touchdown in my career cities with highlights and intercultural insights from the working traditions that have expanded my toolbox. It's there for readers who are interested in the nuances we encounter when we engage across borders. At the same time, the shared learning from each town can be applied anywhere in the world.

Throughout the book I have included examples from my sessions as well as stories about how these skills have made a difference in my own life. In my early years, I certainly didn't have the Right Kind of Loud myself. I was bullied during most of my school years, helplessly different and aloof. I didn't have a voice to connect with others, let alone the confidence that someone might listen. If someone would have told the skinny outsider in the school yard that life was waiting with boundless adventures and that one day people would come to *her* for help to relate to others, she wouldn't have believed her ears. She grew up to become a singer, a performer, and an entrepreneur, enjoying a career that's a true love story. It is my deepest joy to share the tools that helped me get here. My wish is for you to go forth with whatever is in your heart, communicating and connecting your way toward your goals and dreams. May *The Right Kind of Loud* help you leave your mark in the world.

Chapter One

Sound Right

Unleashing the Power of Your Voice

Sound Right

Unleashing the Power of Your Voice

The voice is the muscle of the soul.
—Alfred Wolfsohn

Our language has many examples of the paramount effects of the voice—they haven't found their voice, he doesn't know how to speak up, they were vocal about the challenges, or, in the words of Malala Yousafzai, "I speak not for myself but for those without voice." Without our voice we are helpless preys to people and forces around us. We use it to draw boundaries for what we accept and don't accept. We use it to express our needs and experiences. We use it to lead and show the way. A strong voice is one of the most palpable leadership qualities we can have. And we use it to defend those who are dear to us. Sometimes this can be the key to a vocal breakthrough. One of my voice clients had a voice with a lot of air in it, giving an effect of lack of strength and willpower. We had been practicing different sounds while I was trying to find the one that would make her voice come straight from the gut. Inspired by the two cats in her home and the fact that we were on the twenty-third floor in skyscraper Dubai, I gave her these instructions.

"Place your focus point on the balcony of the building across the road, and there, high up in the air, your cats are balancing on the rail, they could fall off any time. You have one chance to send them your sound, warning them and telling them to jump down." Her voice started softly, gradually growing stronger, and within a few seconds, it was vibrating, floating like a golden stream through the room. For this client, defending her dear ones was the source she needed to connect with her full-body voice. Getting a powerful voice is not about going out on a search for something that you don't have. It's about accessing what is already there. Somewhere inside you, your voice is waiting for you to give it wings. Vocal coaching is simply finding the right doorway, opening up for the sound that is you.

The Voice Is Intimate

From a communication perspective, the voice is the most intimate tool we have. It serves as a bridge between what we wish to say and our listeners. Starting inside the body, your voice is created somewhere in your stomach and torso, traveling upward toward your throat, where various personal and technical adjustments modulate it before sending it out into the air as sound waves. The sound waves then travel through the air before entering your listener through their ear canals, spreading out into their body as vibrations. Think about it for a moment. The connection starts inside your own body, ending inside the body of your listener. It is more intimate, even, than the human touch, entering on a skin level. Few years ago I was reading a novel about a deaf woman who enjoyed going to discotheques to dance. She would place herself close to the loudspeakers, close her eyes, and move to the vibrations. Voice and sound is a physical experience, moving through the skin and landing inside the core of our bodies. Having worked with people's voices for over two decades, I have witnessed again and again how the voice is intimate and personal in a unique way. We cannot be separated from our voice. This makes it impactful and also utterly vulnerable—the voice is who we *are*. The word *person* consists of *per* and *son*; in Latin, *per* means through, and *son* means sound. Through our sound, we become who we are.

The sensitivity and judgment toward our own voice supersede most other communication tools. One of the ways this comes to show is when we start producing different sounds during a voice session. When I ask a client to repeat a sound, I often hear the reaction "Oh, that was really bad." If so, I gently ask, "What did you want it to sound like?" The answer will often be, "I don't know." Even when we don't know what "a good voice" would sound like, we judge the sound coming out of our own throat with an instant reaction.

Almost everyone hates listening to his or her own voice when hearing it recorded. "It's so shrill, I don't sound like that!" The reason it sounds so foreign to our ears is because we are shifting the position we are listening from. When we speak and sing, we hear the sound from the *inside* of our own ear channels, translated directly to vibrations, without leaving the body. And when we listen to a recording, the sound enters from the *outside* of the ear channels, entering the same way it does for the listeners around us. I am often asked what to do about this, and the only thing I can recommend is listen more often, getting used to the quality we hear.

While the voice is intrinsically connected to our identity and who we are, it is also more elastic than we usually think. The voice is often referred to as a fixed entity—*that's just the way it is*. But the voice is much more than one type of sound; it can express every shade of human experience. For those of us who speak different languages, we know that our voice sounds different in each of them. Every language has its own placement in the throat and mouth area, activating different muscles, and this affects the pitch and the overall sound. One of the main advantages of training the voice is discovering that it is bigger and can do more than we think. Our voice is not a fixed entity, but a fluid flow of our aliveness, a unique expression of ourselves in the world.

My Voice Story

I was a nerdy girl with a hungry brain, and like many of us, part of growing up meant getting disconnected from my body. I didn't have the tools to handle a lot of what I experienced, and so, it was easier to stay up in my head, where I could solve things and be in control. If not for a special encounter in my early twenties, I would still have been up there, peering down on the world without presence and wisdom.

I had just arrived in Berlin when one of my friends introduced me to a guitarist from Stockholm. He told me that he had a rock band, and being keen on new experiences, I asked if I could be a backup singer. For a few rehearsals, I found my way to the practice room in the basement at Stephanstraße, but the rock style wasn't really my thing, so I dropped out. For quite a while, every time Gunnar and I met, he would ask me when I was coming back to rehearsals. I used different excuses, thinking he would lose interest, but he kept on asking. One day, when he insisted that I had to sing again, I said, "OK, sure, one day I will, but I'd need a guitarist who wants to play a different kind of songs, I'd want my voice to be heard." Without losing a beat, he replied, "Great, when do we start rehearsing?" I was stunned and flattered and nervous, all at once, this was not what I expected. And so it started. After months of practice, we had our first concert at a backyard party in Kreuzberg. I was so nervous I thought I would faint. My luck that afternoon was a couple of children playing in front of the stage. They seemed less threatening than the cool and hip adults looking at me, so I simply sang to them and somehow it landed well. With our debut behind us, we got even more into it. Our first songs were Swedish folk songs, and soon I dug out my hidden poems from the drawer for us to add melodies and chords. It was an odd thing—a Swedish singer-songwriter duo in Berlin, but people liked us, and I started taking voice lessons to improve my confidence and technique. During this time, my main focus was expressing the stories of the songs. The magic of taking your innermost personal material, dressing it in words and melody, and sharing it with an audience is like nothing else. We performed at small festivals, cultural cafés, and parties, and I learned how to handle audiences of all kinds, from exalted to indifferent crowds.

I left Berlin behind after two years, missing my steadfast supporter and fellow composer, Gunnar. We kept on making new songs and had some gigs in Sweden and Denmark as well, but over time, distance wrapped up our duo. My next voice adventure was waiting in a workshop with a Bulgarian singer in Aarhus. Binka Dobreva knew two words in Danish: *forfra*, which means "from the beginning," and "metal." After two days with this new vocal technique, I was hooked, and I ended up singing in three Bulgarian choirs, perfecting it as best as I could. Then I discovered Ida Kelarova's method of connecting your feelings into the expression of her soulful gypsy songs, making me travel to her hardcore practice ashram in a mountain village in the Czech Republic. Not long after, I heard overtone chanting from Mongolia at a voice festival, and when I stumbled upon a teacher in this technique, I started studying with him. I call them my voiceaholic years. From having been fascinated by sharing my own stories with the voice, I became a disciple of the voice as an instrument, exploring and expanding what it can do. Having been exposed to many voice teachers, I often witnessed examples of unsafe singing environments and saw the effect it had on the students. By the time I started giving my first voice lessons, I knew how important suspension of judgment is for the voice to be released, making me develop an everyone-can-sing methodology. Since then, I've had the privilege of leading choirs and vocal groups in the widest array of contexts, spanning from young drug addicts living in an Alcoholics Anonymous house in Mexico City to team building for governmental institutions in Dubai. Over the years my voice passion evolved into a dedication to support others gain access to the freedom and power of their own voice. The joyous transformation it brings makes me humble every time.

Voice and Words

When we interact with each other, there's often a mismatch between the words themselves and the message of the voice. Here's a conversation between a little boy and his mother that I overheard while waiting in line at the supermarket:

"Mum, can I have an ice cream?"
"No, dear, not before dinner."
"But mum, I really want an ice cream!"
"No, we are having dinner when we get home."
"Please, mum, just this once..."
"I said NO, YOU CAN'T HAVE AN ICE CREAM!"
"Are you angry, mum?"
"NO, I AM NOT ANGRY!"

Just like the little boy, everybody standing in line had gotten the real message that the mother was transmitting, she was indeed angry. And I thought, what an excellent example of the fact that in situations where there is a conflict between the spoken word and the tone of the voice, the tone of the voice always wins over the spoken words.

Already as infants, we start refining our scanning method to pick up the emotional messages of the voice, it's a core part of our survival. And for those of you who have pets, you know how you use your voice range in different ways to communicate with your beloved animal and how it learns to recognize the different messages. This constant scanning between the words and the tone of voice continues throughout our lives, although the nuances become more refined as we grow up and ascend the layers of responsibilities and titles in the workplace. After an important meeting or a date, we often share with someone we trust, "So he said X, what did he really mean?" On stage and on screen, the variations and potential mismatches between the words and the tone of voice are particularly interesting. When studying a role, the actor works with what is called a subtext, the hidden meaning underneath or between the words. A skilled actor knows how to play with the tension, and it is exactly this, the difference between what they say and how they say it, that makes us follow their moves and stay engaged.

As mentioned, the voice is intimate in a unique way because it is created inside our body where our feelings are contained. The instant sharing from one body to another has another effect that increases the intimacy. It's a perfect scan of the emotions we are feeling. Most of us have had this experience when calling someone who knows us really well. We're having a hard time with something, but not really in the mood to share, so we try to hide it.

"Hello darling, how are you doing?"
"Oh, I'm fine, thanks."
"Just *what* is going on?"
"No, really, I'm just a little tired."
"You can tell me, dear, what is happening?"

The first time I understood this principle was after rehearsal with my guitarist in my early twenties. Gunnar was a new friend, and I admired him intensely. In the beginning of our music making together, I would often get self-conscious while my inner critic was attacking from the inside. We were practicing a song when Gunnar suddenly stopped, looking up from the strings and said, "Come on, Kim, you are an awesome singer, stop thinking that you're not good enough, just sing!" I was surprised, and more so embarrassed, being caught in my own saboteur mode. But it worked, helping me snap out of it, so I could change gear and get into the groove. It wasn't until I was walking toward the metro afterward, that I realized the mystery of what had happened. Gunnar could hear what I was feeling and thinking while I was singing! My voice was transmitting the message loud and clear through the melody we were working on, even with other words in the text. It is exactly this capacity to transmit emotions that makes the human voice so powerful as an instrument. Since my realization with Gunnar, I have learned to use it as a tool while listening to countless voices as a coach, picking up on the emotional message to choose the right exercise for each situation.

Vocal Wounds

As a vocal coach and choir leader, I often ask people if they like singing, and sadly, most of the answers I get are negative. "Oh, my husband asks me to be silent." "I really cannot sing." "I'm tone deaf." or the most extreme, "I don't have a voice!" I find this to be a striking example of harsh judgment. You are saying that you don't have a voice—*with* your own voice. If someone asks if you know how to dance, you wouldn't say, "I don't have a body." but something like "It's not my preferred way to move." With the voice comes a special form of vulnerability, and many of us carry what I call a vocal wound.

According to fellow voice coach Tania de Jong, a disheartening 85 percent of all adults have been asked to be silent. It usually happens during middle-school years between nine and thirteen years old, when we enter the social in-and-out groups and try to range ourselves among the accepted ones. Maybe the school choir director asked you to sing silently or mime without any sound. Or someone pointed out that you sang out of tune at a family gathering or in church, and the experience was so embarrassing and sad that since then you stopped singing. The verdict became the one and only truth about your voice.

When we talk about being able to sing, we refer to a very small slice of what our voice can really do. Each culture has its own parameters of how a beautiful voice should sound, limited to a range of melodies and scales sung in a certain way. If you are born in Mongolia, for example, you will be chanting overtones as the one and only way to sing. If you grow up in Bulgaria, you'll be projecting metallic sounds in crashing intervals, and if you come from the South in the United States, your voice will have a twang. The global variations of vocal traditions are a delight of abundance and diversity. When we grow up, however, it is of utmost importance that our own voice matches the voice ideals that surround us. If not, we'll most probably stop experimenting from then on, believing that we cannot sing. The truth is, our voice is much bigger than one single vocal tradition. Both sound qualities and vocal range are elastic and something that can be expanded and explored. The only requirement is a relaxed situation without judgment where we feel safe to experiment.

Another reason some of us develop vocal wounds is a life trajectory with traumas, leading to a disconnection with our bodies. Or it can be the imprint of growing up in surroundings where we are not supposed to be heard, not supposed to take up space, speak up, or question the status quo. Sometimes, the voice is just fine, but the lack of confidence is so deep that it settles into the way we feel about our voice, making us mistrust it.

Vocal wounds and lack of body connection can lead to different kinds of vocal inhibitions, preventing us from getting the message through to our listeners. More often than not, the inhibitions are unconscious, becoming simply the way our voice is. In most cases, a cycle of three voice sessions is enough to amend the issue at hand. Here are some of the most typical ones, I'm sure you've heard a few of them.

Some voices have a lot of air with a fluffy quality around the tone, making it hard to hear and almost impossible to project. In some contexts, this kind of voice is the ideal feminine voice, like the husky voice of Marilyn Monroe. This may be great for movie seduction, but not so great in a professional context. Others have a tendency to keep their lips and mouth area fixed, almost not moving at all when they speak. This makes it difficult for others to hear what they are saying, even more so if you add an accent on top. An effective articulation means having a flexible muscular area around the mouth and soft lips. Then we have people who speak from their head register rather than from the breast register. If you want to sing classical opera, the head register is exactly what you want to develop. For a spoken voice, however, this gives a sense of indecisiveness, as if asking for permission when you speak. Some people have a tendency to only use the upper part of their torso when they breathe, making them hyperventilate in a fast-paced frequency. It can be hypnotic to listen to, like watching someone swimming in big waves while coming up to the surface for air. And some people tend to direct their voice through their nose area, giving the voice a nasal and squeaky quality. Not the worst thing that can happen, but again, it does not signal credibility. Finally, there is a common voice feature that most people don't notice as an inhibition, namely, the place we project the voice from. When people ask me about vocal ideals and a good voice, the first thing I say is that it needs to be body connected. A healthy voice starts from the stomach area, giving a sense of embodiment and depth. As nerves and stress push upward through the body, the voice can easily be pushed upward as well, and it is common to hear voices coming from the throat area instead. The effect is a compressed sound with an intensity that penetrates on a special wavelength, especially when projected with volume. Luckily, the unwanted effects from all these inhibitions are easy to modify with adequate exercises.

Singing is Good for Us

If you grow up with a vocal wound, you are cut off from your voice potential, thinking, or rather experiencing, that you cannot sing. From the outset, we need to be mindful of the way we approach our voice. If we feel unconfident when singing, what's missing is not vocal resources as such, but a favorable situation where the voice can be approached and liberated.

One of the things that happen when we have low voice self-esteem is that we stop listening. As the voice becomes an uncomfortable part of our self, we don't direct our attention toward it, merely accepting the damage. When we start training the voice, the first area to focus on is just that—listening. Before sending out a sound, we need to know what we are looking for. Among all the voices I've had in my hands as a vocal coach and choir leader, I have never met anyone who cannot sing. By using a method that engages the right brain hemisphere, simply done by listening and copying, amazing results emerge in just one session. Another secret to unlocking hidden voice potential is to use songs that are unknown to the participants. In my case, I bring songs from around the world, introducing different techniques and lyrics the participants don't understand. This takes away the inclination to compare with a better or 'right' version of what it should sound like, and from there, it's easier to express, fine-tune, and strengthen the tones.

There are plenty of reasons as to why we should plunge in and reconnect with the innate joy of expressing ourselves with the voice. In recent years, more and more research has been done to verify the benefits of singing, with articles spreading into business publications and social media. Anyone who has participated in a singing session with a group, had a voice lesson, or just sang out loud has felt the well-being spread throughout the body, giving a natural high. When we sing, our brain chemistry changes, as it fills up with the bonding hormone oxytocin, and the neurotransmitter serotonin starts firing up new connections while releasing endorphins, making us happier and smarter. It's like an automatic recharging mechanism, filling the left brain hemisphere with energy and focus, keeping us sharp. And singing affects our health, increasing our longevity. When we do it with other people, the effect is amplified, even making our hearts beat together in the same rhythm. No wonder then, compared to other leisure activities, the sense of bonding and belonging is deeper after singing together. The effects increase even more when singing in front of others, the best thing we can do is to share concert sparks with an audience.

Vocal Elements

The area of vocal training can seem mystical for someone who hasn't been exposed to voice sessions before. How do we transform the sounds coming out of our mouth, at the same time so personal and so fluid? This overview of six different focus areas gives you an idea of what we are aiming at when working with the voice. The impact of sound qualities is nonverbal by nature, and hence some aspects get lost when translated into words. If you would like to have an audio version to support your understanding, you'll find some videos about voice usage on my website.

Pitch—High—Low

From a nonverbal perspective, one of the signals of high status and leadership is a deep pitch. So for the male readers, yes, you have an advantage by nature with your vocal range. However, the most important component of the vocal range is that it isn't too limited. I have worked with several male speakers who tend to hover in a low register that is difficult to hear. Many people think of their voice as fixed inside a certain register, something that is enhanced when we join a choir and are placed as a bass, tenor, alto, or soprano. During my voiceaholic years, when I studied one voice technique after the other, one of them was developed by Ida Kelarova, an outstanding gypsy singer from the Czech Republic. Her voice was soaring up from the depth of earth itself. During her master classes, many of us lost our voice for a while to have it come back with more nuances, reaching into a lower voice register than before. The voice is more elastic than most of us think. As presenters, we want the voice to be engaging to listen to, and a big part of that is making sure we're using a variety of pitches while we talk.

Volume—Soft—Loud

To control projection and volume, both soft and loud, we need support from the diaphragm muscle, placed like a disk in the lower part of the ribcage. I met my first choir director around the age of nine, and he told us to go home, lie on the floor, and put a book on our belly. The instruction was to notice how the book is lifted upward when we inhale and floats downward when we exhale. Another way to connect with this muscle is to notice your body when you laugh heartily. After a long while of belly laughter, you can even feel the connection through sore stomach muscles. If you watch infants, they have the most amazing breath and diaphragm control of all, with their stomachs lifting and lowering in a very visible way.

To project a strong voice, the key is to use diaphragm power instead of pushing it from the throat area. In addition to a great vocal effect, connecting with the diaphragm gives a sense of authority and well-being, as it helps us center in the middle of our body. As a speaker, you can use loud volume to accentuate an important headline or argument. And lowering the volume into a soft voice is one of the most effective ways to heighten the intensity of a message. The whispering quality signals that we are listening to a secret, welcoming the audience into the intimate realm that it loves.

Speed—Slow—Fast

For a speaker, knowing how to control the speed is key. There's quite a variation of speaking speeds in different cultures. Not only the speed itself, but also the implicit agreement around how long we pause when we talk with each other differs. And then we have our personalities—some people take longer time to reflect, while others hardly pause at all.

From a nonverbal perspective, speed itself is an indicator of low status, not wanting to challenge the leader. It makes sense—a leader doesn't have any rush. Embodied calm increases our credibility and makes it easier for others to trust us. When we come up in front of a group as a speaker, our pulse speeds up with adrenaline, preparing us for the "all eyes on me" moment. In itself, the added energy or butterflies in the stomach are healthy, giving us extra focus for the situation. If you're nervous for a speech, and someone says, "Relax, it will be fine," there's a slight misunderstanding. We shouldn't relax, as such. Those extra sparks are necessary to create a special moment with our audience. We just need the butterflies to fly *with* us and not get in our way. And to do that, we need to control the speed and anchor ourselves with pauses.

Warmth—Resonance—Nasal

You might not be familiar with the word "resonance," but you'd be able to recognize the sound of a voice that has it or not without a doubt. A voice with resonance sounds warm and pleasant, making you want to hear more. We create it by relaxing the jaw and the muscles around the lips, allowing for as much space inside the mouth as possible. Technically, what gives a tone resonance are the overtones that are created on top of the base note, the sound we hear. Each base note has its own scale of overtones emerging inside the mouth, and to be created, they need space. You can try a simple version of this effect by singing an open vowel, for example, "oooo." Try doing it with an open mouth, and then lift your jaw, closing your mouth, and listen to the shift in the sound quality. It will sound flatter, colder…losing its resonance.

There's a special technique that concentrates on this aspect of the voice, called overtone chanting. Working with pure sound only without melodies or words, the aim is to project the overtones outside the mouth so we can hear them as separate notes. As they emerge together with the base note, it has the effect of listening to two voices singing together. This technique is a great method to increase resonance as well as develop deep breathing while connecting the voice inside the body. On the opposite side of the resonance spectrum is either a voice that is squeezed by a tight mouth and jaw area or a voice that is projected through the nose, giving a nasal effect.

Articulation—Blurry—Clear

From a communication perspective, an effective voice is articulated with active lip muscle movements. Every language has its own combination of particular sounds, and many of us have a hard time resting the muscles in use from our native tongue when producing new sounds, resulting in accents. Sometimes charming, of course, but often challenging for our listeners. Especially when working in an international environment, active articulation will help you get through to people with other native tongues. If you are a native English speaker, you might want to pay extra attention to this voice element. It's easy to forget the effort other speakers have gone through to be able to express themselves in a second, third, or maybe even fourth language that their English might be. The best way to practice articulation is simply by copying foreign sounds in songs, rhymes, and poems, or if circumstances allow, repeating words people around you are saying, all the while keeping it playful and fun.

Expression—Intense—Neutral

We have a physical dislike toward voices that are neutral and flat. Being a direct transmitter of feelings, we don't like it when there's nothing there. The worst examples are synthetically produced voices, like long phone menus with "Your call is very important to us," making us cringe. There's something about our human connectedness to the voice that makes us extra sensitive. We can hear what another person is thinking and feeling in the tone and sound of the voice, and for communication purposes, we want our voice to be expressive and alive.

An Effective Voice

While every voice is unique and different sound qualities might be desirable, from a communication perspective, there are three criteria to consider:

Body Connection—Imagine sitting in a group of people practicing vocal exercises. You're listening to a voice that has been struggling with body connection. When it finally clicks into place, you'll recognize it immediately. Maybe the voice was coming from the chest or throat area, maybe the person was speaking from the head register, or there was a lot of air in the voice. Whatever is going on, when listening to a voice that lacks body connection, we naturally feel a yearning for it to land. It's like a homecoming, both for the person who is sending the sound and for the people who are hearing it. The quality to be sought for is centered and warm, a tone that has strength.

Voice Elasticity—Monotonous voices with a flat intonation are the least attractive to listen to. We start thinking about other things, we get distracted, we fall asleep. Elasticity is needed to make the voice dynamic and engaging. It can be in volume and projection, in pitch from high to low, in expressivity, or by using different sound qualities.

Voice Expression—This is more important than anything else. Even a voice that is projected with inhibitions hits home as long as it is connected to the feelings of its sender. There is no one way of speaking with an expressive voice. It comes naturally when you are comfortable with yourself and engaged in your topic.

Voice Tips for You

Step out of judgment. I had a voice client recently who came with a low voice self-esteem. She had grown up in a country where children were not supposed to be heard, and her experience with the school choir was embarrassing, leading her to conclude that others can sing, not I. After years of repression and feeling that something is wrong, leaning in to hear what the voice has to say before using it can be a way to start. The first task I gave her was to create a ritual for her voice. I asked her to find a peaceful space to sit and listen inward with a silent enquiry, maybe a message would emerge? She came back and shared how she got an impulse to contact someone she knew and say what was on her mind. She had been holding back because the message was her intuition speaking and she couldn't find any apparent reason to support it. Reflecting with me afterward, she shared her revelation: "'I don't have to justify myself, speaking my truth has a value in itself." When we step out of judgment, the voice becomes our ally. Find a way that suits you, and approach your voice with curiosity.

Start experimenting with your voice and explore what it can do. Many years ago, I was contacted by a high-end finance adviser in the world of B2B deals. He wanted all the tools I could give him to excel in client interactions. Our first sessions were dedicated to the voice, and soon he found himself reproducing strange sounds he had never heard before. During the second session, he suddenly asked, "Why are we doing these exercises?" Trying to explain, I used the image of our two hands and the task of giving a handshake. Although the range of muscles in use for a handshake is limited to small movements, the way to strengthen its power is by making a big circle with the arm. If you do this with one hand and not with the other one, the hand that has been extended into its full range of possibilities will have a different presence during that same handshake. The same conditions can be applied to our voice. By extending our experience of what it can do, we obtain a different quality when we return to our normal speech.

If you drive to work, sing along to your favorite artists. If you are a parent, sing with your child. If you sing in the shower, let it flow. If you are outside, sing to nature. There's an ancient vocal tradition from Korea called "story singing," where practice would include singing against waterfalls, in caves, at ocean waves, and to mountain's echoes. Let yourself be inspired, any time and place that allows you to use your voice is a good time to use it.

Join a choir, or take some voice sessions. One of my clients was a soft-spoken medical doctor who joined a postgraduate in women's leadership with my voice sessions. We had a couple of group sessions and an individual one. Here's her account of what happened: "I can't remember when I started to have a conflict with my voice. As years passed, I realized that it had turned into a kind of rebellious resident, not accepting the orders from my mind. And so I started mistrusting it, and when I felt betrayals coming, I kept it locked inside. One day I found myself in a voice session, doing things I had never done with my voice. By the end of the session, each one of us was singing a song by ourselves. My voice was flowing—powerful, beautiful, vibrating, truly mine. Now I realize, our voice is a reflection of our most authentic self. And I am progressing: During two important meetings last week, my presence was improved, and I could make myself heard naturally. The before and after effect of the training is immense." The good news is that most of us only need a few sessions to heal a weakened voice, making it body connected and strong. Try it out when you have the next chance.

Chapter Two

Move Right

Glowing with Your Presence

Move Right

Glowing with Your Presence

The words a leader speaks are important, of course. But *how* they're delivered can make all the difference, especially in tough times.

–John Baldoni

When humans get together in groups, be it at a conference or a party, small clusters gather around certain individuals. The feeling we get when we enter the room is, "Oh, I wish I was her." or "How can I get close to him?" Looking closer at these magnetic individuals, they aren't necessarily the most beautiful or handsome person in the room, and their formal ranking might be anywhere on the scale that is setting the standards of the gathering. What these people have in common is that they are comfortable being in their own skin. This allows them to tune into their aliveness and engage with people around them in a relaxed way. They have what we call presence. If you want to touch that magic and increase your charisma, you've landed just right in the field of nonverbal communication.

Statistics—It's a Lot

One of the most famous research projects in this field was done in the sixties by Professor Albert Mehrabian, who was working at UCLA. By testing people's reactions to different words and images, he measured how much of their communication signals were verbal versus nonverbal. He concluded with some striking numbers many of you will recognize from other books on body language. Before I continue, let me add that there are many versions of this result. The simplification of the experiment frustrated Professor Mehrabian to such an extent that he published an afterword to his own research, lamenting the way it has been misused. What he had measured were the signals showing what we feel about the message we are communicating, not the message itself. With this in mind, the question goes—how much of our feelings are revealed through our words? It is merely 7 percent. All the rest, 93 percent are nonverbal signals. And of these, a big chunk of signals represent the way we use our voice, namely 38 percent.

Other research in the field has shown the difference between the speed of our facial expressions and our consciousness registering what is happening. When we talk to each other, we are sending a constant stream of nonverbal signals, confirming how we are receiving the words we are hearing. We don't think about it, it happens automatically. The time it takes for the facial expressions of the listener to adjust to the message that is received is three-tenth of a second. For our consciousness to become aware of that same message, we need five-tenth of a second. The speed of the nonverbal reaction is almost twice as fast!

The Gut Brain

The body's seat of emotional connection as well as nonverbal communication is in our stomach. It's in our language, we sense a decision with our gut feeling. When we are nervous, butterflies fill up the belly, and in Swedish, we advise each other to have ice in the stomach for challenging situations. The ancient Asian cultures with their martial-art traditions have had this knowledge for thousands of years. Across the different disciplines, the basic body position has the stomach as the center point. If you practice the art of qigong, a Chinese medicine tradition with movements and breath, the "qi" or "chi," meaning the vital energy of the body, is placed right underneath the navel. By now, western science with research centers like Johns Hopkins Hospital in the United States and Max Planck Institute in Berlin have caught up, finding an autonomous nervous system inside our intestines that controls functions like perception and immune processes. It's been named the gut brain or the stomach brain, and it works like an intake for the nonverbal signals we pick up from people around us.

The connection to our gut brain is essential for us to notice what we are feeling about our own reactions. At the same time, we use it to interpret nonverbal signals from others. Without this connection, we cannot decode the signals and include them in our mental consciousness. Because the sensations are just that, nonverbal, we sometimes refer to them as intuition or a sixth sense. I'm the last person to deny that we have a sixth or even a seventh sense. However, many of these perceptions are simply nonverbal signals that haven't been integrated into the mental brain. Not surprisingly, the word "intuition" comes from the Latin verb *intueri*, *in* meaning "upon" and *tueri* meaning "to look." We "look upon" the nonverbal signals we are receiving, giving us a sense of knowing.

When it comes to the communication between our mental brain and our gut brain, research has shown that the amount of data flowing upward from the gut to the head is about five times as much as the information flowing down from the head to the gut. Think about it. The seat and receptor of nonverbal communication is placed in our gut. This information registers almost twice as fast as the mental consciousness. And the amount of nonverbal information flowing upward compared to the verbal flowing downward is almost five times as big. Our transmission of nonverbal signals, communicating the emotional charge about our own messages, covers 93 percent of the signals that we are sending. It's a lot. It's fast. It's ongoing. If we want to be effective communicators, we need to integrate the wisdom of our gut brain, both as receivers and senders.

The Big Head

In the information age, most education and career activities have an overly mental focus, and so, many of us develop what I call a disproportioned head with a tiny, little body dangling below. As a result, the little body underneath will undoubtedly feel some kind of pain or exhaustion. Maybe the shoulders are saying "I am so tense, I need to stop typing," or the stomach has vague sensation of discomfort after a conversation, saying something about not trusting the other person. Or maybe the body needs rest, not uncommon, as many of us are sleep deprived. In situations of pressure and deadlines, we try to get as far away as we can from these messages by disconnecting from the body. So, in addition to being disproportioned, the head and the body are often cut off from each other. The imbalance causes some handicaps. In this state, it is really hard to concentrate and stay focused. We lose time and precision by looping back and forth with our attention. Another disadvantage is the effect on our presence or charisma. A person who has that magnetic *something* is someone who brings gut and head together while interacting and being. And when we are in this state, it's easier for others to push us into doing things we don't want to do. Imagine a Western soldier with the energy center of his body in the chest. And then imagine a Japanese samurai with the energy center in his stomach. If someone tries to push them, they will react differently. The Western soldier will easily lose balance and stumble to one side, while the samurai will bounce back to center, leaning into the axis of his body. As shown by this physical image, when we are disconnected from our gut brain with our energy center in the head or in the chest, we are more vulnerable and susceptible to manipulation. To access our values and set our boundaries, we need our whole self, all at once.

One of the easiest ways to get out of an overly mental state and help our body and mind connect is breathing in slow motion. While there's no right or wrong around what specific technique to use, the guiding principle is to do it slowly. By going down in speed, we open the inner flow of energy between the body and the mind, with our neck and throat serving as the highway between the two. Asking my participants during sessions what they do to connect their body and mind, I have received various suggestions. Leaving the desk to walk around the block can be a great way to refresh. Working in the Middle East, some participants shared that they connect during praying time. Others, by doing yoga, Pilates, or meditation. For you to start out, here's an exercise that is designed for us to move from big head to balance and presence.

Breath of the Bull

This breathing exercise has some special benefits in addition to the body-mind connection. By expanding the body with air and lowering the head into a samurai position with the center in the middle of the body, you are resting in the most powerful body position you can possibly have, with a readiness for whatever comes at you from the outside world:

1. Place your feet parallel under your hips, feet pointing forward. Move your knees slightly to make sure your kneecaps aren't locked. Adjust your pelvis slightly forward so your bottom is tucked in. If you have tried martial arts or dance techniques, they use this same starting position. In Pilates, they call it "the neutral spine", it's a tiny movement. Roll your shoulders a couple of times to relax them.
2. Find a focus point with your eyes, and tilt your head forward while looking straight ahead, so your chin is covering your throat. It might feel a little tense, like almost looking up through your eyebrows. If so, you can do the breath with closed eyes as long as you keep looking at your focus point behind your eyelids. It might be easier to concentrate with your eyes closed. Both versions are fine.
3. Inhale slowly through your nose, and let the air fill your body like a pillar, starting between your legs and spreading upward throughout your stomach and chest. Notice your body expanding when the air enters, all the way up to the shoulder blades on your back and your rib cage on the front, making a big space for the lungs. Be aware of tensions; it's a soft sensation, like an inner massage of air, no pressure.
4. Hold your breath for an instant. Sense the feeling of strength and natural authority. You may want to place your right hand on the ribs on your left and vice versa to gain calm in solar plexus, and feel the torso expanding and as you inhale. Be careful not to create a tension or use too much power when keeping your breath, it should be a short instant only before you exhale.
5. Keep the upright position while exhaling through your mouth. While exhaling, let your jaws drop and be loose and relaxed. When exhaling, don't use any force, let the breath go without control.

Practice Tips

Can be done almost anywhere. By taking three breaths once a day for two weeks, the exercise registers into your body like an inner presence pill for you to use when you are tense or nervous about a high-stake situation. Before a meeting, presentation, or call that is extra important to you, find a private space and do three bull's breaths to ground yourself. This quiets the stressful voices inside your head and helps you enter with full presence.

Body Language as a Whole

I've come across many books and articles presenting body language as a kind of alphabet with different gestures and their meaning. While a lot of it might be relevant, in some cases it can be an oversimplification of nonverbal communication as such. Crossing your arms, for example, is often quoted as closing yourself off from your surroundings. However, when we interpret body language, we receive the messages as a whole, landing in one simultaneous instant. And in this "whole," we include all kinds of factors that help us adjust the meaning of what we see. Maybe the person you are watching is cold because of too much air conditioner in the room, simply crossing the arms to stay warm. Or maybe it's a way to relax for this particular person. I once knew a professional speaker who would captivate his audience from behind his crossed arms, to him the position worked as a way to ground himself.

At the same time, there is a level of nonverbal communication that is universal. One of the pioneers in the field, Dr. Paul Ekman, ventured out with a group of fellow researchers in the sixties to test the hypothesis: Are facial expressions different depending on where you are born and the cultural conditions that you learn, or are they the same? Having studied people's reactions in an isolated tribe in Papua New Guinea, they were able to conclude that human beings have a common set of feelings and facial expressions that come with them. When you experience victory, like crossing the line at the end of a race, you show it with the physical impulse of raising your hands in the air. Even if you are blind and have never seen someone do this gesture, you will do the same. It's part of our universal human behavior.

In addition to this universal behavior and its signals, other layers are added to the mix. Whatever we do with our facial expressions and body is also personal. Some people have a discreet way of talking, while others use their hands and arms a lot. To evaluate a situation, we need to know what the personal baseline looks like. And then, there's the contextual factor. We change the way we interact in different situations. Talking with a stranger, a family member, a colleague, or a child, you will display your nonverbal signals differently. Lastly, we have different codes for what a good behavior looks like from the culture we grow up in. In Sweden you are not supposed to raise your voice. Whatever happens, you try to keep a friendly and neutral tone. In many Asian cultures, looking someone in the eyes is inappropriate if you are speaking to a person who has a higher rank or is older than yourself. In the United States, the spoken voice is generally loud. For Scandinavians, for example, their speaking style in public transport can be disturbing. And in collectivist cultures like India, the space between bodies when you interact is small, making it acceptable to move up really close to the person you are talking to. This can be provoking for someone who comes from cultures where you have a larger personal space. When we interact with each other, these layers mix into one impression with universal, personal, contextual, and cultural signals all at once, adding to the complexity of our interpretations.

On a Mammal Level

Returning to the universal level of nonverbal communication, there's another master in the field who is worth mentioning. As a zoologist, Desmond Morris started by studying animal behaviors for many years, until one day, he turned his gaze to what he called "the human animal." With an evolutionary and biological approach combined with an open mind, his observations are remarkably interesting, even more so as he manages to suspend any kind of judgment while describing his findings. In his book, *The Human Zoo*, he looks at human behavior in the big cities. The title refers to the fact that a modern city is far from the jungle we often call it. In a jungle, the animals have plenty of nature around them, moving freely in all directions. In a city, however, we are boxed in, living, working, and being transported in small spaces or boxes, just like the cages in a zoo. Comparing human behavior to that of different animals when they are trapped in a zoo, the book takes you on a journey of behavioral insights.

One of the focus areas is status behaviors. As Morris puts it, these behaviors are just as valid for baboons as for presidents. Every time a group of mammals gather in a room, one of the animals will be the leader, while the others display a nonthreatening or submissive behavior, showing that they will stay out of conflict. At the same time, there's always a level of status tension in the room. What if the leader gets sick, who will be the next in line? And in situations without a clearly defined leader, another kind of tension will fill the air while different individuals try to make a bid for their domination of the group.

High and Low Status

The behavior of a leader and the nonthreatening others is demonstrated by what we call high and low status signals. Before taking a closer look at how they appear, we need to make a distinction between the nonverbal dimension and the high- and low-status attributes on a societal level in different groups of humans. For example, living in Dubai, it's easy to see that having a luxurious car is a sign of high status. But when I think of my community in San Francisco, the opposite is the case. For them, leaving a low carbon footprint and being conscious of the environment is high status, and many of my friends pride themselves on taking public transport and biking when they can. We tend to forget that our own status depends on what group we associate ourselves with. In reality, there are myriads of different high- and low-status rankings that we enter and do our best to rise within during our lifetime. Keeping in mind that personal, contextual, and cultural aspects vary, the following overview is a guideline for high- and low-status signals on a nonverbal level.

Head and Eyes

When I ask participants what we do to signal high status with the head, I often get the answer that it's tilted upward, putting the chin out in front of the face. This particular gesture is actually not high status from a nonverbal perspective, but a cultural gesture that has been added on. Going back to the big head, we know that a powerful posture has a connected body and head with the center in the stomach, even tilting the head forward to protect the throat like a samurai. Imagine that you are trying to get the attention at a meeting where many people are talking. Try raising your hand and shove out your chin while saying, "Excuse me,

I have something to add." Now try to do the same while keeping your head in a normal position with a relaxed chin covering your throat. Do you sense the difference? By pushing your chin out, you are willing to leave your center to attract the attention of the people around you, signaling that you don't think they will listen. By staying with your head centered, you are drawing the attention toward you while keeping a high-status position.

Moving to the eyes, there's a signal that shows submission in a split second. By looking someone in the eyes and swiftly looking down or away and then returning with the gaze, we are clearly not going to threaten the person we are meeting. The flickering eyes also indicate this by being a fast movement. If you want to signal that you can be trusted and relied on, this is not recommended. When it comes to how long we keep looking someone in the eyes, various cultural codes have different ideals for what is appropriate. As a rule of thumb, resting your gaze in the eyes of the person you are engaging with for longer moments, will signal a relaxed high-status that is sympathetic to interact with.

Arms and Hands

I am often asked what to do with the hands when giving a presentation or having a conversation. If you are self-conscious, and you don't know what to do with them, it's fine to place your hands calmly in front of you while holding them together. This way, they are not in the way, and they don't attract any extra attention. However, in most cases we use our hands to illustrate what we are talking about in a natural way, and if this works for you, it's what I recommend. The more we express with our body when we talk, the easier it is for the audience to follow us. For example, if you mention three different points, you can easily show one, two, and three fingers for the audience to *hang* the argument on.

There's another guideline to be mindful of—don't keep them under the waistline, and if you sit by a table, don't keep them hidden. It can create assumptions about you trying to hide something. Sometimes I am asked about keeping a hand in the pocket while talking. I usually don't recommend this as it's a relaxing signal, and in most cases, we want to come across as alert and engaged. However, in some contexts, a relaxed approach can be preferred, depending on the audience and the speaker.

Legs and Feet

For the whole body in general, opening up and straightening your posture signals high status, while closing yourself in and making yourself smaller shows low status. One of the indicators is the position of our feet. By turning them slightly outward and opening our legs, we show high status, while turning them inward, we do the opposite. In many contexts, crossing the legs is a preferred position, and it doesn't necessarily indicate low status, although it is a way to close the body. This is another example of cultural layers added on top of the nonverbal signal.

Touching Yourself

You might have noticed in some conversations that people touch themselves. For women it tends to be their hair or neck, while men sometimes touch their belly or arms. This body signal usually happens when we are tired or overwhelmed. It's the body's way to say, "I've had enough of impressions today, and I need some time to be with myself and digest." Not terribly bad, one might think, but definitely not desirable in interactions where you want to come across as engaged and in charge. When done in nervous and fast movements, like fidgeting or twitching, touching yourself is a strong indicator of low status.

Speed and Pace

Of all the body signals we send, the overall high-status signal comes through a calm demeanor and not acting too quickly. The reason is simple—a leader has no reason to be nervous or stressed. As a leader, you know how to handle any challenge. You will take care of it, or your entourage will. By speeding up, on a nonverbal level, you are signaling that you're not feeling in charge. A leader who comes late doesn't rush. He or she walks calmly into the room, others may wait.

There's no automatic alignment between a formal position and the nonverbal signals we are sending. Sometimes a mismatch can create an awkward tension. One of the most common situations this might happen in is during presentations. As an audience member, we're part of a contract where we are supposed to be silent and the speaker is to lead, and when we see someone up there struggling with nerves, it feels uneasy. And sometimes we come across a person with low ranking on an outwardly social scale, showing a behavior of inner leadership. I've had my share of taxi drivers and security guards in Dubai making me humble with their dignity.

The Status Swinger

So, for us to be effective communicators, what is the best way to use these signals? Contrary to what some might think, walking around in a constant high-status position is not desirable. If we have two people going at each other where both are striving to keep the dominant upper hand, what happens on a nonverbal level is almost like a freeze. While both keep escalating, it's increasingly difficult to reach an understanding. For this kind of situation, I recommend to soften up and move into a lower-status position for a while. This will allow the other person to relax a bit, and in most cases, the dynamic can change back, for you to be in high status again.

I've had some participants who protest when I share this, saying that they would lose face if they don't hold on to their high status. Some contextual and cultural codes might indicate this, of course, but as a rule of thumb, even the greatest leader knows how to adapt to different situations. It takes a solid level of confidence to apply this flexibility. You need to trust yourself and your ability to lean into different modes of interaction. The strongest high-status position is shown by not holding on to it too hard.

In some situations, your speaking partner might be so low in status that it's difficult to interact and extract the information you need. For example, during an interview with a candidate, if he or she is too nervous, a lowering of your nonverbal signals can help him or her relax and gather focus again. And then there's a special kind of situation that requires our ability to swiftly change into a low-status behavior, namely, interactions with professionals like police officers or security at the airport. People who take on these roles are usually sensitive to their ability to stay in high status, and it's unwise to challenge their need. I've had many experiences of success when encountering these kind of professionals by voluntarily sliding down into an obvious low status, making the other party relax, and sometimes even loosening the rule they are about to enforce.

In other situations, a clear high-status position is the desired approach. When someone is about to give you a responsibility, you'll make them doubt whether they can trust you to take ownership and complete the task if you are showing low-status signals. In most first-time encounters, interviews and introductions, a relaxed high status is advisable, not to be confused with an imposing high-status approach that leans into arrogance. Sometimes we're placed in an involuntary low-status position that it can be tricky to swap out of. One of my clients was struggling with a manager who was talking down to her, making her feel insecure. If this happens, instead of defending yourself, a better approach is to go into consulting mode with comments like "I understand this is important to you, tell me more about X…" As you're talking, it's crucial to relieve the tension that builds up inside from feeling disrespected. When we have an emotional trigger of discomfort, we usually try to repress it. By doing this, the impulse simply stays somewhere in our system, ready to bounce back when we least expect it. It often comes in the form of an outburst to the wrong person, making us lose even more status. A helpful metaphor to counter this effect is the image of making the body bigger. By expanding ourselves and giving space for the sensation, we are able to access our assertiveness while maintaining a calm appearance in high status. The *Breath of the Bull* exercise in this chapter is helpful for this purpose as well.

There's a special kind of situation where a high-status approach is absolutely necessary, and that is when someone is reaching out to you for help or comfort. When someone is sad or upset, telling you how worried he or she is about a relationship or a job situation, for example, the best response is to be soothing and calm the other person down, even if you don't know how to solve the situation. This is especially true if you are relying on this person to complete a work task for you. When we are in an emotional state of emergency, our frontal brain cortex where we process data is momentarily blocked, so you are wasting your time with whatever message you are trying to deliver, until he or she has had a moment to recover. After this you can continue where you left off. In addition to saving time and gaining efficiency, you are improving your relationship with the other person by supporting him or her.

During my years as a trainer with these skills, I only once encountered a participant who had issues going up into high status. It was a young business student from Germany, and in his head, he was associating all kinds of high-status behaviors with dark leadership. On the other hand, I have seen plenty of examples of participants who have a hard time going into low status with their body signals during role-plays. It's a good exercise. As part of the human experience, we all play multiple roles, and the more flexible we are when interacting with each other, the easier it is both to get our message across and to gain empathy and understand what the other person is going through. Knowing that you can bounce back and forth with your status is the ultimate goal for a confident communicator, enhancing your presence.

Lie Detection

One of the questions that often comes up in sessions about nonverbal communication is, "How do I sell a product I don't really believe in?" My answer is simple. Try to find another product, or say as little as you possibly can and avoid talking about things that are contradictory to your convictions. The reason being, unless you are a professionally trained actor or poker player, your body signals will reveal that something is off. As stated in the beginning of this chapter, when we interact with each other, nonverbal signals make up a major part of our communication. A big part of them are our facial expressions and micro expressions. The reason they are called "micro" is because they are expressed at a very high speed, involuntarily exposing a person's true emotions. To see them we need to watch a video recording of the face in slow motion. The same Dr. Paul Ekman who investigated whether nonverbal communication is universal or culturally conditioned, came to the conclusion that we have a set of basic emotions, each with its own universal facial expressions. These are the ones to focus on when we are trying to assess the accuracy of people's words. Some people have a natural talent in this field, picking up signals that go by unnoticed for most untrained eyes. The good news is, we can all practice and get better at it. To start out we need a baseline, observing how the person we are talking to is expressing him or herself when speaking about something neutral. In an interrogation, for example, the interrogator uses some time to establish the baseline before going into specific questions he or she wants to test for potential dishonesty. What we are looking for when evaluating truth or lies are not specific signals as such, but a discrepancy between different signals or between the context and the signals. If your words are saying that everything is fine while your hand is clenched in a fist, there's an obvious mismatch. We can see that something is not right. Or, if someone is behaving like a family person in a courtroom, something is strange.

If you feel pressured to say something that isn't right for you, remember that the sensation of being honest or not doesn't come in gray shades. We don't perceive each other as usually honest and sometimes dishonest— it's either or. Ask yourself whether the thing you are about to say is worth the risk of being placed in the category of the dishonest. Typically, with the effect that your listener will start doubting all the other things you have shared. When we evaluate the level of honesty of other people, we are using our gut brain. After an encounter with someone who is sending off contradictory signals, the way we know is that vague sensation in our stomach about something being strange. Connecting back to the beginning of this chapter, our most important tool when it comes to interpreting nonverbal signals is right there, making it even more important to connect our minds and bodies so we can pick up the signals from the gut brain.

It's kind of ironic to be writing this. If my younger self could read this chapter, she would have been baffled and probably protest. By anchoring my identity in my intellect, I was closed off from so much of what was going on. Today, I won't do anything without consulting my stomach brain, and I know that the wisdom resting there far exceeds the power of my mind. Some of you have experienced it. In extreme or dangerous situations, the mental brain doesn't have a chance to process fast enough, it's the gut brain that saves us. I would not have been able to conquer distant countries and markets as a woman on my own without a solid connection to my gut brain. It is this inner knowing that has allowed me to be brave and take risks that many wouldn't dream of. In addition to guiding me in decisive moments, my gut connection gives me confidence and presence, both invaluable tools for my career as a communication trainer.

Chapter Three

Listen Right

Winning People Over

Listen Right

Winning People Over

Do you listen, or do you just wait to talk?

*—Mia Wallace (Uma Thurman)—*Pulp Fiction, *the movie*

Of the two communication acts, listening is often considered to be the passive one, while speaking is active. It's actually the other way around. Speaking equals thinking out loud and doesn't require a lot of focus, while listening demands both intentional attention and practice. I call it intentional because, even though we want to, it is challenging to stay with other speakers and the words streaming out of their mouth. We usually speak at a rate of about 150 words per minute, but our minds can process information at a speed between 300 and 500 hundred words per minute, giving us the opportunity to fill in the gaps with associations and thoughts about other things. In addition, our general capacity to stay focused has decreased severely in the last decades. Many jobs require a prolonged state of multitasking, tearing on our concentration muscle. While multitasking is possible, multi-focus is not. And to listen, we need to stay focused with our whole self.

Less Than a Goldfish

Microsoft did an investigation of the average human attention span, measuring the result of twelve seconds in the year 2000. By 2013 it had landed at merely eight seconds, one second less than the average attention span of a goldfish! The reason for the decline is easy to spot. It's our increased interaction with technology and especially the swapping back and forth between different interfaces and screens, tearing on our capacity to concentrate. The results resonate with me on a personal level. During the writing process of this book, I've been noticing how tempting it is to have a glance at LinkedIn or check my emails to get that rush of gratification that a "like" or a new greeting gives. More and more discipline is required to stay with our eyes on a page and not switch over to another one. In an age where we are bombarded by information and messages, getting through to someone is far from easy. And once we have the attention, we need to work even harder to keep the other person engaged before they zap on through their day. Navigating through this landscape, redundant information feels like noise, it's almost painful on a physical level. We don't want information. We want others to research our interests and tailor whatever message they have to be exactly what we need. What we crave, consciously or unconsciously, is for someone to be interested in *us*, for someone to really listen.

When we are talking with someone, we assume our words will make sense to the other person. We commonly use around 5000 words in our core vocabulary. Many of them have 20 to 25 different meanings, so two people with a 5000-word vocabulary can easily sit in a field of over one 100,000 different alternatives. The fact that we have expressed our thoughts by sending off words into the air does not necessarily mean that we have communicated. Meaning isn't created inside our own head. It occurs when the receiver manages to make sense of what we have said.

And the only way to make that happen is by listening. Actively. If you think this sounds easy, simply try the exercise of repeating what someone else has said after a few moments of speaking stream, no longer than two minutes. Not giving your version of what the person said, but repeating the meaning of what was presented. I've done this exercise with many different groups and profiles, every time with a surprise in the room, when the level of challenge is experienced hands-on. I even had a group once that got slightly aggressive when confronted with their lack of listening capacity. It was for an MBA in corporate communication, where the participants had a self-understanding as superb communicators, having been handpicked as experts in the field. It felt harsh, but it was for their own good. The first step toward becoming a good listener is to acknowledge how unusual and difficult it actually is.

Elephants and Realities

The first time I came across Active Listening as a method was in the classroom at Copenhagen Business School, where Professor M. Capek from New York was giving a summer course in management communication. He opened the class by promising that this skill would change our lives. "If you start practicing now, you'll start sensing the difference in a few months. People will like you more. Your colleagues will want to work with you in a new way. Your relationships will improve." My first thought was, how American, typical exaggeration. Then I started practicing, living the method. I was wrong. Real listening changes everything.

There's an ancient fable from the Indian subcontinent about six blind men who came across an elephant for the first time. Each of them was touching a different part of the elephant's body. One had the tail in his hand, thinking it was some kind of rope, while another was holding the trunk, making him think of a snake, and so on. When they started describing what an elephant was, their versions were completely different, leading to a fight about who among them was right. The moral of the story is that humans have a tendency to create his or her version of reality from a limited experience and perspective, forgetting that we only have partial information.

And that's where listening comes in. We don't know what part of the elephant or reality other people are holding. The only way to find out is to pause our own version and listen. When I come in to support around different communication knots, I often hear the comment "But I said so!" The saying itself isn't communication. For that to happen, we need to concept check with feedback from the other party, making sure that what we said makes sense to them. In addition, we select and filter what we experience through our preferences. If you have decided to buy a red car, you'll be struck by how many red cars you see in traffic in the coming days. Our mind notices the things that we are focusing on. This goes for conversations as well—we hear what we are listening for. Which is why it is so important to start with a blank slate. In Japan they have a saying: "cleansing your gaze," for the act of giving each object a fresh look without assumptions and expectations. This is what we're aiming for with our ears when we start a conversation. When we talk, there's a lot of stuff going on. The theater world calls it the subtext, the underlying need that drives a person to do something. Practicing for a role, one of the initial exercises is to read your lines out loud with different subtexts, deciding on the one that fits your interpretation. There's a cushion of possibilities under every sentence. A good listener is tuning in to hear more than the words, trying to catch the stories between the lines. Here's how you do it:

Active Listening Method

1. **Pay attention to the meaning of what the other speaker is saying; pay attention to body language.**

Open yourself to take in the speaking person, the words that are said, the unspoken ones, and the nonverbal signals with body language, facial expressions, and tone of voice.

2. **Let no meaning escape you: clarify, summarize, paraphrase.**

This step requires some courage. In our daily life, we skip a word or two that we don't understand when we read or listen, letting the context and the story fill in the blanks for us. When applying this method, we need to stop and ask about every single word that we're not completely sure about. It can feel a little embarrassing. We don't want to seem stupid in front of others, and it takes quite an oomph of energy to interrupt someone in the middle of a sentence. For us as listeners, it can feel impolite and even a little violent. The interesting thing is that for the person who is speaking, the experience is positive. To them, your interruption tells them that their message matters to you, increasing the rapport between you. Nevertheless, you'll probably need to practice this a few times before you get used to it.

3. **When you notice that your mind has wandered, *instantly* return to the speaker's meaning and body language. Do this as often as necessary.**

Notice that this paragraph starts with "when" and not "if." It happens to all of us, no matter how much we try to stay focused. Our mind is so elastic and swift, it takes practice to quiet it down and stay tuned. The trick is to not judge ourselves the instant we notice that we have wandered off. When we get upset, a stream of negative thoughts is unleashed, taking our mind even further away from the speaker and making us lose out on more of what has been said. The way to go is to be soft with ourselves and simply return with our attention and a short "Where were we?" You'll get to practice self-acceptance as well as listening, repeating this as many times as needed.

4. Pay attention to what you say—*as* you say it—*not before* you say it. Do not rehearse your next remark.

This is a challenge for everyone who has an associative mind, meaning pretty much all of us. You're listening to someone who is telling you about his Italian grandfather from the North of Italy. And you immediately think, "Ah, I have to tell him, my Italian neighbor from Milan is such a great guy, maybe he knows him somehow, I have to ask!" And then your conversational partner continues talking about other things. The only issue is, you don't have a clue about where he's going, because all that you are doing is sitting there, waiting for the next opportunity to interject with the special connection you felt to your Italian neighbor. Maybe the conversation has gone on to something that is far more important than a potential neighbor acquaintance. Maybe the other person has opened up a hidden chamber, daring a trembling jump of trust. Maybe he has continued with updates about his wine export of Chianti, which could have been the perfect match for your newly opened restaurant. But you don't make the connection to potential wine import, because all the while this was happening, you were sitting there, waiting to get your comment in about your Italian neighbor, afraid that you would forget your association.

For me personally, this instruction is almost spiritual—it requires faith. To be able to let go of your associations, you have to trust that, if it is important enough, it will come back to you. You have to believe in the mastery of the moment, however many ideas you need to let go of to be present. If you have that competitive bug, challenging yourself with how long you can continue without waiting remarks inside your head can be an excellent motivation while you learn the skill. The mantra goes: if this thought is really important, it'll come back to me. What is he or she saying again?

Now that you have the instructions, you need to find your own way to apply them. Have a close look at the four steps above and summarize them into simple key words that work for you. For example: focus— ask— return—trust. Then write the words on a note and place it somewhere handy where you can reach it at any time, like in your calendar or notepad. The idea is to have them up your sleeve so you can activate the process by a quick glance. To get into action, what you need are some juicy practice situations. The trick is, we cannot practice these skills with someone we know and like. In friendly situations where we want to listen, it usually flows pretty well, and if we lose attention for a while, no real issue arises, because the connection can be repaired easily. What we are looking for are situations where we *don't* want to listen, the heated moments when we disagree with someone, feeling triggered and provoked. Maybe someone comes to mind as you're reading this, a colleague or family member with whom you have a hard time. If so, you can plan to bring the four-step method with you next time you're seeing that person. Other situations you can plan to use the method are meetings and networking events or potentially boring dinner invites—all great training arenas. You'll get the most out of it by putting the method into action when you're thinking to yourself, "I wish that person would shut up!" The goal is to bring an inner trigger detector, telling us to start exactly when this happens. If you are the slightest bit like me, you'll fail many times. It is far from easy to shift focus when we are irritated, stressed, or upset. Throughout the many years I have been passing on this method, only once have I come across a participant who couldn't apply my practice instructions. He was a young finance broker in a prestigious banking firm. When I told him to seek out difficult communication situations to apply the method, he sat silent for a while before telling me that he didn't actually have any in his life. Incredulously, I inquired a little more, but he was right. Maybe it was his heritage, being adopted from an East Asian country, he had something of a young Buddha in his energy field. And he did have an exceptional flow in both career and private life. I bowed to his capacity of seeing other perspectives even when opposing his own. However much I'd love to say the same about myself, I still have some distance to cross before I get there. My life keeps giving me plenty of practice moments. And for us who do, the time frame to start out with is short. Professor Capek recommended ten minutes three times a week, and then, when you get more experience, you can increase slowly. It's a good idea to have a date set three months or so later, and check in with yourself and potentially with a colleague or friend, to see if there's a noticeable difference.

Early Ear Openings

Having the capacity to listen and take in the people we meet on our way is more than a skill set. It's a way of life. Growing up as the daughter of a musician, I was helped along to develop big ears from an early stage. Malcolm played the French horn at the opera, and distinguishing this sound among the other instruments was one of the first things I learned.

One of the stories from my toddler days is about me climbing up the stairs and suddenly putting the forefinger in front of my lips while calling out "Shhh, daddy!" I was convinced that all the French horns in the world were blown from his lips and everyone should listen when he played.

By the time I was a few years older, he would sometimes take me by the hand on trips to the city, where we would visit the opera and do errands. To get there, we would use T-banen, the Oslo Metro, and while walking through the metro corridors under Jernbanetorget, he would stop and talk to a man who was selling postcards from his wheelchair. To me, it was a mystery, my father talking to someone who could have been a stranger. But through their conversation, it was clear that the man in the wheelchair and my father had become friends. The air around them when they talked was filled with affection. They were sharing as two equals, and the moment was one of importance. I thought for many years what he was showing me that time was how to talk to strangers. Then one day I realized, what he was role modeling was a true listener's approach.

Curiosity as a Doorway

The best fuel for your listening capacity is real curiosity. When you are truly interested in someone, you don't need to work that hard on it. I found a doorway to this treasure box while doing the oddest job in my early twenties. While working night shifts at the central post terminal in Stockholm, a bunch of newly hired were offered the chance to apply for the railway post, internally called the Navy SEALs of the postal workers. We would embark late evening and sort the mail by different zip codes into small compartments on the wall while the train rolled its way through the nocturnal landscapes toward Malmö. Once in a while, the train would stop at a station and sacks with mail would be handed off and new ones loaded on board. This summer was the second year ever that women could apply. The railway carriage was a man's world with sturdy originals who had developed their own little pocket of a universe.

Wearing my new safety shoes as part of the uniform, I started my late-night journeys as the only woman in my shift, entering a social scene completely different from my artsy circles. We had hours ahead of us on each trip, and when the final destination was close, we would turn a plastic box on its head, spread a postal sack over it, and play cards. So what do you do when closed in on a train with time to kill and a workload that is ebbing back and forth? You start having conversations. At first clumsily feeling my way, I got to know these men from another world. And somewhere that summer while the train tracks sent rhythmical beats into the night, I realized that everyone has a doorway to shared magic if you ask the right questions, no matter how different your lives have been. If you don't have anything obvious in common, imagination does it. It's all about putting yourself into the shoes of the other person—How would it feel if it was you?

The doorway of curiosity has helped me ever since, especially in networking situations. When meeting someone for the first time, we're flooded by impressions, most of them nonverbal. In the midst of decoding and often with one part of us taking in the room and gauging where to move next, a real intention is required to become present and tune in to listen. If you do, the reward is palpable. By picking up on what the other person is saying and feeding it back with a relevant reference, something beautiful happens. It's almost like watching a flower opening in the face of your speaking partner. And you'll find the person remembering you, wanting to help and connect you on. The networking situation is one of endless examples. Of all the communication skills, your ability to listen will help you most when it comes to influencing people around you.

Listening Within

In a fast-forward world, we often find ourselves tugged away from listening, feeling that we should be somewhere else. Mindfulness teacher Tara Brach talks about how easy it is to be distracted by our own agenda. And when talking with others, we often get caught in our reactions of judgment and criticism. Getting through those levels of inner noise requires both compassion and self-kindness. Just a few weeks after starting to write this book, I visited Gandhi's Museum in Mumbai. Among the items that moved me most was his quote about listening. To him it was a lifetime practice. "There comes to us moments in life when about some things we need no proof from without. A little voice within us tells us, 'You are on the right track, move neither to your left nor right, but keep to the straight and narrow way'. I have developed some little capacity to hear the still small voice within clearly, and I shall lose my usefulness the moment I stifle it."

Sometimes we are afraid, hiding from that inner voice and the truth it might bring, making it even harder to receive the messages from people around us. To truly listen, we need to clear away the noise, layer by layer. In whatever way it suits you, try to find a way to strengthen your attention muscle both toward yourself and the people you interact with. During a talk I gave some months ago, a young audience member raised her hand and said, "Attention is the new currency." I agreed and added, "Yes, attention is the new currency, and listening is fluid gold."

Chapter Four

Speak Right

Engaging Your Audience

Speak Right

Engaging Your Audience

**People will forget what you said,
people will forget what you did,
but people will never forget how you made them feel.**

—Maya Angelou, American poet

The easiest way to evaluate a presentation is by looking in the eyes of the audience members. If they are glowing with sparks, you did a good job. Every encounter with a live audience has the potential of that special magic with vibrating presence in the room. And every audience brings a wish for the moment to be relevant, to be worthwhile. It is up to us as speakers to answer the prayer of the audience and make it so.

I often start my presentation sessions by asking, "How many times have you suffered as an audience member?" And when I do, the air is full of hands. How can this be? Well, public speaking is an unacknowledged art form. For some reason, this ability is often believed to be something that we are born with. But learning how to give effective presentations is a skill, just like learning how to drive a car. No one gets on the road without lessons or at least some practice with a co-driver. There is a slight exception and that's if the person is raised in the United States.

Growing up in this culture, getting up in front of people to represent your class, your club, or your company is a natural thing, giving them a head start. Even so, mastery requires practice, and when you see someone shine on stage, it's because he or she has done it many times before. At the same time, the fear of public speaking is almost archetypal. Having coached hundreds of speakers, I can testify that the vast majority of us are entering the stage with nerves that threaten to take over our focus.

Why Are We Afraid?

Learning how to become an effective public speaker is all about expanding our comfort zone. To engage the audience, we need to bring our whole self along, and we need to feel good about ourselves and the situation. I sometimes use the image of bringing a big round piece of carpet to stand on when we deliver our talk, like a safe zone that is all ours. One of the most amazing examples I have seen of someone doing this was during a talk in a high-school gymnasium in Albuquerque, New Mexico. By one of those small miracles, I had landed in the United States the same morning, and the friend I was staying with knew someone who could get us tickets. And so I came to see Obama addressing the crowd during his campaigning days in August 2008. His presence and elegance was striking. Even during hostile audience questions, he remained completely at ease, making the whole room with all of us in it his comfort zone. You might think, gosh, I cannot be as good as Obama. The good news is you're not supposed to be. The goal is for you to be as good as *you* are, bringing your whole self to the occasion.

What makes it difficult to bring that whole self along is the lack of feedback from the audience. When we are in face-to-face conversations or talking in an intimate group, we receive a constant stream of signals from the others, confirming how our words are landing with them.

Their facial expressions and gestures keep telling us whether they are interested and whether they agree or not. When we talk on the phone, this feedback turns into apparently insignificant sounds like *mmm* and *aha*, guiding us through the conversation and helping us adjust along the way. We are so dependent on these signals that if the line is silent for more than a few seconds, we immediately reconnect with, "Are you there?" When we enter the stage as a speaker, these conditions change. Suddenly we are confronted with a number of potentially blank faces, and our pauses linger in the air without any sounds to support us. In the silence, our inner critic gets activated: "I haven't prepared enough," "Can they see how nervous I am?" "What are they thinking of me?" I once had a particularly irritating audience member frowning skeptically right in front of me on the first row. While doing my best to ignore him, my frustration kept on throughout the talk, why did he even come to this event in the first place? To my surprise he came up to me when the talk was over, eager to discuss. It had been one of the most fascinating talks he'd ever heard! His expression had simply been one of deep contemplation. We never know what is hiding behind a neutral face. As part of the contract between the speaker and the audience, the speaker is the one who needs to be generous in expression.

Grounding and Sacred Pauses

When we are about to walk out in front of an audience, an extra burst of adrenaline kicks in, often turning into nerves. Their physical journey travels upward from our feet, beginning with trembling knees. I remember some of my first concerts, when it felt like the dress was moving from side to side like a sail in the wind. The next body part for the nerves is the stomach, filling up with butterflies. If the nerves intensify, the chest will start heaving as we hyperventilate with short gasps of air, and for many people, the most sensitive part of the speaking moment is the voice itself, as it starts trembling or breaks off. If the pressure continues, the nerves will block our brain with a blackout, the worst-case scenario for many speakers.

It's a misconception that we should be calm before an important talk. We often say, "Just relax, you're going to be fine," but the nerves are part of the extra spark that sharpens our presence, we need them for our audience connection. The art is knowing what to do with the butterflies, we want them to fly *with* us and not block our sight. The best approach is to counter the upward flow of nerves by grounding yourself. What you can easily do *before* the talk is to take some slow-motion breaths while connecting with your stomach and the center of your body. *During* the talk itself, imagine that your breath is coming from the soles of your feet, anchoring your energy downward. A good way to integrate this is to draw a symbol in a different color between the key words in your presentation notes or at the bottom of your slides, reminding you to stop and breathe between them. Another thing you can do is reconnect with the reason you are there, what is it that you want to tell them, and why is it important? Or you can connect with the audience in front of you, what are their needs, and how will your topic be useful for them? The trick is to get out of our own self-consciousness and connect with what we want out of the situation. Another effect of that extra adrenaline kicking in when we walk on stage is our inner speed picking up, making us speak faster. On a nonverbal level, any speediness is low status, while high-status behavior is calm—there's no rush for a leader. To manifest your leadership in the room, you can apply what I call the sacred pause. There are several reasons why this makes you a better speaker:

Grounding

As mentioned above, the pause is your chance to calm your nerves by anchoring the energy downward while you imagine the breath coming from the soles of your feet.

Increased Attention

Listening to a stream of words while trying to stay attentive is hard work. If a voice goes on for a long time without any breaks, the effect can easily be hypnotizing, soothing us into a sleeplike state. By pausing, you give the listener a chance to integrate what has been said and, at the same time, a refresher before the next point is made. And for potential listeners who have lost their attention already, a pause gives them a chance to refocus.

Translating Layout

When we look at a written text, the layout with titles, fonts, and paragraphs helps us digest the content. In contrast, when we listen to someone, all these support functions are gone. To transfer the layout into the speaking stream, using pauses is the most effective way to mark a title, a phrase that's bold, and transitions between sections.

Dramatic Effect

The pause is one of the best ways to add gravitas to your message. When something dramatic or high stakes has been said. Pause. When you are moved and want your audience to connect with the feeling you are displaying. Pause. When you receive a question that is provoking or spot-on or in any sense big. Pause. The pause increases your leadership and authority in the room, letting your message land inside your listeners.

Stories and Emotions

The thrill of storytelling is stored in our DNA. Since the dawn of civilization, we have gathered around the bonfire, listening to stories about our ancestors and myths about the world. It's become part of our physiology and the way our brains are wired. A storyline helps us learn and remember what we have heard, making it easier to convey whatever subject we wish to deliver. When the audience picks up that a story is coming, it joins together in a simultaneous leaning in, just like the Disney impulse of tiny animals, cuddling up when Snow White or Cinderella starts to sing.

To create a story, what we are looking for is a specific event or situation. If we use general terms and words like "always" or "never", the audience cannot enter into the story. In the fairy tales, the magical phrase is "Once upon a time"—it is *one* chosen moment. Think of the beginning of a movie. During the first seconds, the camera will display some kind of environment with images and music, showing the audience where the story is taking place. And then, after a while with shifting sceneries and names scrolling by, the camera zooms in on a person, signaling that the story is starting with a close-up. When we speak, the same thing happens. While the camera uses a close-up with the lens, we create the same effect by using our senses and filling the moment with details. What did it look like? Were there any significant sounds or smells in the air? What were you thinking? Sometimes the context around the event will add a spice to the story. Maybe the time period was a historical moment that people relate to, maybe the geographical place adds a special meaning, or maybe you are sharing from a life phase that many of them will remember.

When you include different people in your story, like your father, your mentor, or your manager, use real names. The difference between "my father" and "my father, Anton" is huge. With the name, there's a sound to connect with. Maybe someone has an Anton in his or her life, maybe they have never heard this name before, it doesn't matter. A name opens the door to a deeper level of intimacy. As a speaker, it takes an extra jump of giving away something special, inviting the audience into your life. To them, it feels like generosity and realness.

And then we have the piece about emotions. When it comes to public speaking, the fear of being transparent, as in "they will see who I really am," is a paradox. We tend to think that the formula for a good speech is based on acting like a professional, transmitting information in an organized way while staying as neutral as possible. The truth is, to connect with your audience, there's no better ingredient than the use of emotions. It's the feelings that grant us credibility and the ability to win an audience over. During a workshop, an executive MBA student protested when I shared this. He said that while his superiors could get away with this, it didn't apply to his own presentations. The contextual factors vary in different organizations, of course. Nevertheless, part of what makes someone a leader is the ability to step into their role and show up with authentic presence, conveying who they are and the values they care about. My advice to the MBA student was, start observing the presentations of your leaders and let yourself be inspired. It's by filling our role with passion that we pave the way to senior roles while expanding our circle of influence.

Five Preparation Steps

When we are assigned to give a presentation, most of us start out by thinking about the topic, "Do I know enough, what kind of research do I need to do?" The *what* keeps swirling in our head, often for a long period of time. And all the while, this is not the way to start. Here are the five steps you need to prepare your presentation successfully. Do note the sequence, the order they come in is crucial.

1. Who—the Audience

Start by asking—Who am I going to talk to? What are their needs? Are they interested? Are they skeptical toward me as a speaker, or do I have credibility? Is the topic new or is it a repeat theme? What is the context for the presentation, and what kind of space will the event be in? You need to know this first. Establishing your audience awareness is paramount for an effective presentation. Your audience will notice within a few seconds whether you have done your homework. This preparation step also makes it easier for you to gain confidence. If you don't know your audience beforehand, try talking with someone who will be there or someone who knows the typical audience profile. And if it's a high-stakes presentation and within reach, visit the venue beforehand. It helps your body to take in the space while imagining the audience in front of you, like the recalibration of an instrument. The more you know about your audience, the easier it is to have success with your talk. Here's a checklist to get you going:

- Context—work, meeting, conference, event
- What are their needs—concerns—interests?
- Volunteer presence—or "asked" to be there
- Expectations—what do they know about the message?
- Is the topic new or repeat?
- Are they skeptical—can you meet that at the start?
- Your reputation—what do they know about you?
- Relevancy—is this the right content for the right moment?
- Duration—potential delays—tech support
- Space—comfort—air condition—seating—refreshments

2. *Why—the Objective*

The second question is—Why am I doing this? There are many different objectives when you give a talk. It is never *only* to inform, although this is what most people answer when asked about the purpose of their presentation. If this were the case, it would actually be more effective to send an article in a PDF file. But while an article may be informative and clear, it lacks the opportunity to engage with your audience. When we give a presentation, in addition to passing on information, there's a wish to influence. The intention can be to brainstorm, to make a decision, to share a point of view, to entertain, to address skepticism, to motivate, to mediate… In most cases, the objectives come together in different combinations.

As part of your preparations, you need to know your specific objectives. To identify them, ask yourself—When I have said my last word, what is the sensation that I wish my audience to sit back with, what kind of impulse would I like them to have? Is it a feeling? Is it a reflection or a question? Do I want to change their behavior? Do I want their names at the bottom of a sign-up sheet, or do I want them to buy my services? Knowing this will help you align your preparations as well as help you establish the success criteria for your presentation. If you have an audience ally, someone you know in the audience whom you can trust to give honest feedback, you can ask him or her whether your intentions came through.

3. *What—the Content*

Having found the *who* and the *why*, it's time to ask—about *what* am I talking? Do note, this is preparation step number three, not number one. The first two questions will inform you about what kind of research you need to do. When you approach the what, be mindful of the duration. The shorter your presentation is, the more difficult it is to stay within the time frame. If your time slot is under ten minutes, you need to rehearse with a timer at home. The most common presentation mistake is including too much information. How many times have you heard a speaker say something like: "Really, we should have had one hour, but we only have twenty minutes, so I'll have to rush." And how does that make you feel? What's missing in this case is synthesizing—the ability to identify the core message in a large quantity of data and make it appropriate for the allotted time. Whatever amount of information that you are assigned to deliver and however big your passion is for the topic, your task as a speaker is to make the presentation digestible and hopefully entertaining, even in situations with last-minute adjustments when you are given half the time you were scheduled for.

As an audience member, we program ourselves to bring our intentional attention for a certain amount of time. And when that time is over, the attention has been used up, pretty much like a battery. Passing the time limit is unforgivable if you want to make a good impact on your audience. There are some exceptions. Sometimes unexpected things happen, maybe some juicy questions took the discourse into a new route, maybe half of the audience arrived late due to traffic issues, or if you're super engaging, maybe they just don't want to let you go. Then what you can do is renegotiate by asking if you can have some more time. Most audiences will be thrilled by the fact that the speaker acknowledges the end of the time slot and happily grant you the extra minutes you're asking for. If you try this, let the people go who have something they need to attend, so they're not kept as hostages while their child is waiting at the nursery or their boarding time is ticking away. Remember, though, the best result you can strive for as a speaker is leaving the audience wanting more.

4 How—Structure and Design

The how is everything you do to get your message through, starting by separating form and content. For the purpose of this preparation step, we are looking at the form aspect only. Another way of saying it is, when you are a good speaker, you can make any content interesting—the soup your aunt makes every fall, your latest combats at work, the reason you get provoked by comments about happiness. Consider how to start and end, potential interaction with your audience, duration for each segment, transitions between them, and design of the visual aids you'll be using. Here's a checklist you can use:

- Introduction
- Conclusion
- Transitions and duration
- Audience interaction
- Questions
- Visual aids—slides—three-dimensional props

If you have limited time to prepare, make a choice about the introduction and the conclusion. I mean literally knowing the first and last sentence that you're going to say. Then go through your material, and ask yourself if there's a way to show the audience what you want to tell them by using an example or a story. In most cases, the clarity of a presentation is heightened by one deep example as opposed to many superficial ones while sacrificing some of the data. Consider if there's a place where you can engage your audience with an exercise of sharing in pairs or open-ended questions that can add to your credibility. If you are using slides, ask yourself if they are truly visual and not just bundles of text and if you can drop some of them. Death by PowerPoint is a well-known condition, and at some conferences today, slides are even forbidden as an initiative to develop real speaking capacities and audience engagement.

5. Delivery—Fine-Tuning Yourself

When we enter the room, our body is telling the story about how we're feeling… about ourselves, about the people we're meeting, and about the message we are carrying. And yet, this final preparation step is something most presenters never get around to. The difference between someone who includes it as part of their preparation practice and someone who doesn't is palpable, not least to yourself. It accounts for everything that helps you calm the nerves and bring your whole self along, including choosing an outfit that you are comfortable with and that suits the occasion. Any kind of body connection and well-being moment is recommendable. You can do breathing exercises, listen to some special tunes in the car on your way to the venue, or have a delicious meal before you arrive. One part of being a good speaker is being able to let go of the script. The more present you are, the more flexible you can be, adjusting yourself to the needs of the moment. It's all about being generous, giving the audience as much as you possibly can. And for you to be able to do that, you need to give yourself something before you start. You need to be generous with yourself.

Bathing in Yourself

This exercise was designed to help you charge your batteries of body presence and well-being prior to your presentations. The idea is to find a state where you are feeling fabulous, not because of anything you know or achieve, but just for being you. While doing it, it's forbidden to think about your talk or anything you need to do afterward. The activity should be safe and relaxed. This is not the time to try out new things, it's about repeating something that is guaranteed to make you feel great. Here are some examples to get you going.

One of my clients from Dubai loved dune bashing, driving in the desert on a four-wheeler. It's a great one, and I told him he might need an alternative, as there will be times in his life when he has a high-stake presentation without access to the desert. Another client had to improvise her bathing in herself moment as she was delayed with everything those last twenty-four hours before her conference. The way she did it was simply by arriving earlier to the hotel and finding a table by herself in the lobby, where she had her coffee and a moment in silence. More than doing something exceptional, the power of the exercise lies in telling yourself that you're doing it. Sometimes it can be challenging to fit it in. At one point I was helping the best wine taster in Spain prepare for the European championship. We practiced each category, and I came to learn quite a lot about this exclusive discipline. I had no idea that decanting the wine at the right angle and choosing the perfect cigar after a meal can be measured and judged! When I asked him what he did to relax, he couldn't think of anything. With the coming competition, his family, and a full-time job in a restaurant, there was no time for himself. I kept asking, and after a while he revealed that sometimes, when he came home after a long shift at the restaurant around 3:00 or 4:00 a.m., he would sit and zap through the TV channels before going to bed, always with a bad conscience. Considering the pressure this young man was under, the last thing I wanted was to add more to his to-do list. My instruction for his bathing in himself moment was simply to zap through the TV channels for twenty minutes before falling asleep when he had the impulse—and feel good about it. Having those relaxed moments for himself in the midst of contest categories and demands was a pivotal part of his success in front of the jury.

There are endless versions of this exercise, the more physical your moment is, the better. When you step out in front of your audience, the body is your vehicle of communication. The body has a short-term memory, so it's optimal to do the exercise within the last twenty-four hours before your presentation. Reserve fifteen to thirty minutes as your special time, and make sure you are alone when you do it. If you invite someone else, you are risking that you will be distracted by their needs rather than concentrating on your own. Besides, the moment you step out in front of your audience, you will be alone. During those fifteen to thirty minutes, your task is to breathe in the sensation of how wonderful it is to be you. Spoil yourself in any way that you can, buy that very nice bathing salt that you love or a new shirt, or take the car an extra mile to a view of the bay and look at the horizon, whatever it is that you need to make this your time to feel great. Finally, just before giving your presentation, find a place where you can be alone and take a deep breath, reconnecting with the sensation of well-being. It will help you relax so that you can tap into the presence you need to give your utmost. Because the moment you enter the stage, it's not about you anymore, it is about *them.*

Q&A as Leadership Tool

For many speakers, one of the factors that scare the most is the questions their presentation might give rise to. And it's for a good reason. It is not uncommon to watch a good presenter plunge ahead to suddenly lose ground when the discourse is interrupted. When a hand comes up, you can feel a heightened attention in the air. Will the reply increase the relevancy of the topic and help the speaker connect with the audience or will it do the opposite? With every question, you have a unique potential to use the Q&A as an influencing tool to demonstrate your leadership. Here's how:

1. Repeat the Question

There are two reasons for this. Most often there are people sitting behind the person who is asking the question, meaning that the rest of the audience didn't hear it. You are also checking whether you understood the question correctly. There's nothing more irritating than a speaker who misses out on the question and starts talking about something else.

2. Eye Contact

Start by having eye contact with the audience member who is asking. It's a reflex to look a person in the eyes when we are talking one on one, so you'll do this automatically. The moment you have picked up the question and confirmed that you have heard it correctly, instantly take your gaze away from the person and bring your eyes back to look at the whole audience. Your answer is relevant for everyone in the room. You don't want to turn your answer into a dialogue between the person who is asking and yourself. When you have given your reply, return to the person who asked and look him or her in the eyes again. Sometimes a short glance and a nod is enough to confirm that the question has been answered. Other times, you might want to make sure by asking, "Did this answer your question?" If you choose to do so, you have to be ready to deepen your answer and develop it further, so have this in mind before you go there. On rare occasions we are confronted with malevolent questions that have a different purpose than actually deepening the understanding of the topic. It can be a question to provoke you, to demonstrate that they know more than the speaker, or in the most common case, someone raises their hand to simply hear their own voice. If you are confronted with this kind of question, take your eyes away from the person who is asking and interrupt them. It can feel rather violent the first times you try it, but really, you are only fulfilling your role as a presenter, which includes being the leader in the room. As the one in charge, you can do it graciously while getting back on track and continue your talk with a smile. The trick is not returning with your eyes to the person who posed the question. If you do, this nonverbal signal means that the person can continue their word flow, and believe me, he or she will! Managing this, you have saved yourself and your audience from being hijacked by an audience member rambling on about something irrelevant. If you open your senses, you'll feel the waves of gratitude from your audience, while your credibility and leadership have been strengthened.

3. Stay on Topic

When you receive a question, do your best to give a brief answer and don't start a new talking point. The audience cannot remember the question that was asked for a very long time, and everyone is waiting for the reply. If the question inspires you to launch into a new topic, make sure you introduce it, so the audience can follow your train of thoughts and knows where you are going.

4. Answer Right Away

In some situations we have a designated time slot for Q&A at the end. If this isn't the case, it's best to pick up the questions immediately. When one hand is in the air, that person is representing several other audience members, and you are risking talking to a room full of wandering minds, waiting for the answer. In addition, you are missing out on the opportunity to deepen your audience connection during your talk.

5. Be Honest

If you don't know the answer to a question, say so. There are many elegant ways of doing it—you can politely say that you'll investigate and return with the results, or you can refer to sources where the data can be found. The context you're presenting in will tell you what kind of reply is adequate. The first reason for sticking to the truth is the mere fact that your audience will not believe you if you don't. Already as young children, we learn to trust *how* something is said and not the words themselves. In addition, when you are speaking to a group of people, you are typically standing in front of them, and part of the contract between the speaker and the audience is the permission to look at the speaker without pausing. While exposed, your nonverbal signals come through even stronger than during a meeting or a coffee conversation. Unless you are a professionally trained actor, these signals will give you away in the moment of any camouflage. Secondly, the qualities of authenticity and integrity are at the very core when an audience member evaluates the relevancy of a presentation. Think about it from their perspective. When you sense that the speaker is avoiding something or putting out false facts, are you interested in the rest of the presentation? While sharing this with a handful of financial directors at a pharmaceutical company a while back, one of them nodded fiercely. In a situation where he didn't have the exact numbers, he made a compromise in his answer. As a tax expert, his credibility was key to any client interaction, and it took him quite a while to recover.

Questions are not disturbances taking you away from your topic, although they can sometimes feel like it. An audience member who poses a question is a gift. It takes both muscle power and courage to interrupt your word flow, revealing a real interest to make sure he or she can get back on track when something is missing. Usually we speak about a topic we know a lot about, and in favorable cases, we are even passionate about. Under these circumstances, it's increasingly difficult to take in how our words are received. We're speaking from inside our own bubble, often with nerves, making it even more challenging to open ourselves to feedback from the audience. A question is your chance to adjust and increase the relevancy of your topic. If you handle it well, it can be the biggest boost ever up on the podium. As a rule of thumb, there's always a possible audience connection in a question, and the effect of answering it successfully is worth more than the amount of data you might have to give up because of potential time loss. When you handle your Q&A well, in addition to clarifying your content, you are demonstrating your leadership in action, leaving them hungry for more.

Chapter Five

Tell It Right

Writing Your Story

Tell It Right

Writing Your Story

No matter what you do, your job is to tell your story.

—Gary Vaynerchuk

Whatever career direction you've chosen, a big part of it is going to be writing. Emails, reports, memorandums, proposals, social-media posts, and more emails. And of course, any educational endeavor includes some bigger chunks of writing as well. Some of us like it just like that—the process, the words, the sharing opportunity. And then, many of us really don't. As it happens, the way we have been exposed to writing during school days often leaves an uninspired memory with an overarching focus on avoiding mistakes.

This is sad for several reasons. Research has proven that the mere action of writing down our troubles has a healing effect that can be measured in a strengthened immune system and reduced body pain. And there's more to it. While engaging with the empty page, unknown truths and stories emerge, allowing us to make sense of our life. When we write, not even the sky is the limit; we create our own reality, deciding… everything! Inspired by my studies at Biskops Arnö Writing Academy in Sweden and writing guru Natalie Goldberg, I developed a process designed for you to establish or recuperate your writing self-esteem. This kind of writing is for your own pleasure, naturally strengthening your capacity to express yourself while developing your own writing voice.

Guidelines for Creative Writing

This method uses "starters," the first words of a sentence, for the writer to continue on. It's different than the titles we used in school essays. A typical one would be "Summer Vacation," and the whole text had to be about the summer, ending with a conclusion. The starter works as a bullet point for the writer to shoot off from, and the text can go in all directions and land anywhere, no specific ending is required. Here are some examples: "I will never forget…" "In the beginning…" "I'm dreaming of…" A short time frame is recommended. Try it with five minutes, and then expand to longer time slots. When you have chosen your starter, apply these guidelines until the time is up.

Keep the hand moving—don't stop!

In creative writing we need to leave our keyboards and use a pen over the paper. In itself, it's not that easy as many of us hardly write by hand at all. It's almost mystical, but something happens when we write by hand, and it's not the same when we type. The movement with the hand and the arm activates the stories that are hiding somewhere inside our bodies, creating a pathway word by word. Often the fascinating parts are hesitating a little—it takes a while for the connection to be made. If we stop, the connection to those inner stories is broken and we have to start off from scratch again. You'll see what I mean when you read some of your own texts using the method.

If stuck, repeat the last word or starter sentence

If we're not used to nonstop writing, the impulse to reflect and look for the right word or the next passage comes easily. When it does, a good strategy is to repeat the first phrase that you started out with. In addition, to keeping your hand moving, this often creates a nice effect for the topic you are writing about, giving you a chance to explore it from different angles. Another tool is to simply repeat the last word you were writing until a new impulse comes along. "I was coming home with a strange sensation, not knowing what to think...think...think...think...No one had talked to me like that..." It might feel awkward; no worries, you can always edit redundant words out afterward, but the connection with that inner story stream is only there in the moment—it's crucial to continue.

Turn off control and censorship, "think" with your pen

The idea is to get the words straight down onto the paper without any considerations of what it might sound like. Usually we reflect and make choices of what words to pick when we write. For this method, all of them should come straight down through your hand. During my workshops, I sometimes hear texts with sentences like "Kim is asking me to keep writing, and it feels like it's all irrelevant, I'm just doing it, and..." It shows that the method is applied, helping the hand to stay in motion. Soon it will open into the spaces where hidden gems are waiting.

Use your senses, use details—Show, don't tell

By using our senses, we invite the readers to relive the text together with us. Anything that smells, sounds, looks, tastes, or feels helps the reader activate known or new sensations inside. Don't shy away from details, they bring us closer, like a camera zooming in. An apple is not just an apple—it has a size, a color, and a texture. Is it a Granny Smith or a Red Delicious, and where was it grown? If someone is afraid, show us what it feels like. "The boy opened the door with a squeak, his heart was beating so loudly, the sound was filling the whole room. Suddenly he noticed that his hands were moist with sweat." The opposite would be "The boy opened the door. By now he was really scared." As readers, we don't like to be told what is happening, we prefer drawing the conclusions ourselves.

If foreign words pop up, keep them

For those of us who speak more than one language, words from different ones tend to pop up when we start writing. In my case, shopping lists and notebooks have a mishmash of six, so I know how useful this guideline is. When a word in another language comes, write it as it is and continue the sentence. If we stop to check in a dictionary, the flowing connection to those inner stories is interrupted. The translation can be found later, in the editing phase. Sometimes keeping a word in a foreign language adds spice and flavor to a text. For the readers who know the other language, they are delighted to recognize the word, and for the readers who don't, they are meeting a new sound to be filled with word wonder.

Don't think about grammar and spelling

This can be challenging, especially if we are language nerds who like getting it right. The thing is, when we start looking for the right verb conjugation, we are activating our left brain hemisphere where analysis and linear time reside, and this writing method comes from the right brain hemisphere, where feelings and sensations are dwelling in one eternal now. To encourage the discipline and stay out of editing mode, a limited time frame is necessary. And writing in a group is really helpful. Being one of many, with the only sound in the room coming from pens moving across paper, the impulse to stop for spell-checks is easier to resist.

Write hard and clear about what hurts

This is a quote by the author Ernest Hemingway. I include his advice to encourage you to let whatever emerges come forth and keep on writing without judgment. When I facilitate creative writing sessions, the next step after writing is reading the texts out loud to each other, and this can feel scary. On the one hand, it gets personal, and on the other hand, we often don't know what was streaming out of us during those nonstop writing minutes. It can be quite a surprise to read your own words afterward! If you have the opportunity to try it in a group, you'll experience how the unique becomes universal and vice versa. By going deep into our most intimate experiences, we make them accessible for others to relate to, right across whoever is participating. Likewise, the universal becomes unique when you hear how differently everyone responds to the same starter sentence. The reading round will leave you in awe with a hands-on experience of the mysteries inside each and every one of us.

In addition to strengthening your writing confidence, creative writing helps you tap into your right brain hemisphere, where your creativity is seated. It's a great brainstorming method for innovation processes and collaboration initiatives, allowing the participants to deepen their bonds through writing and sharing their texts. I have also used it with people who don't see themselves as writers, helping them access a voice that hasn't been heard before.

Writing through the Walls

At one point during my career, I was carried high by inspiration from sessions in creative writing at various educational institutions. Asking myself where it would be most uplifting and useful to share these tools, I came up with the idea to conduct writing workshops in prison.

After many requests and dead-ends, I ended up being invited to Vridsløselille Statsfængsel, one of the biggest state prisons in Denmark. It was a male-only prison where most of the inmates served long-term sentences after serious crimes. The building itself was like a movie setting, constructed in the eighteen hundreds and mighty like a fort with an entrance tower and massive brick walls. Once inside, it became real very fast. After a rigid security process and leaving my cell phone behind, I was guided upstairs into a tiny room with a stripped-down interior. Under a small window and a blackboard on the wall, a handful of tables and chairs were thrown together. Already in their seats, seven pairs of eyes observed me closely as I entered. Their faces seemed closed off, and one of them had a menacing expression that scared me when I looked his way. I set out with my instructions as usual, asking the participants to share a text or book they had liked in their life. A rugged old man with a thin face hiding behind a long beard mentioned the title of one of those learning-how-to-read books from primary school. My heart sank. He probably hadn't read anything since then. How would I make this experience valid for them?

As part of my preparations, I had received the advice to include myself as a participant. This turned out to be crucial, allowing me to become a fellow writer in the room as opposed to someone talking down to them. We used starters such as "I am…" "What I left behind…" and "The biggest lie…" The biggest challenge was having the inmates give each other feedback in a respectful way. I soon realized that these men knew a minimum about each other. The reason for their prison sentence was a secret for sure, and the atmosphere between them was one of distrust and tension. You could almost cut slices of bitterness and accusations in the air. At the same time, I knew that the sharing rounds were crucial for the experience to land. By using strong boundaries and a readiness to jump in when someone crossed the line from text comments to personal remarks, I was able to make it work. I'll never forget the thin old man reading in a cracked voice about the harsh conditions on the farm where he grew up. The words were simple, just a few lines. Even so, the breakthrough was unmistakable, his chest heaving as he read out loud. It was as if he was hearing his childhood self speak for the first time since he was that little boy.

After three workshop days together, I stumbled out, exhausted. I had never been exposed to such a violent environment before, the sarcasm between them, sometimes lashing out on me. It was raw. To my surprise, I was contacted after a few months and asked if I would come back for another course. This time, I was equipped for the conditions, and we had a remarkable writing journey together. Of all the exercises, the one that is engraved in my memory was the time we wrote a poem to our fathers. The inmate who initially had scared me with his gaze read his lines with tears streaming down his face, while everyone sat in silence. Walking out through the prison gate, I made an inner bow to the courage these men had shown me. Their outer walls were still closed, but somewhere inside, the inner ones had a softening and some new dents.

Crafting Your Bio

We all know it, the question that keeps coming at us as we navigate through conferences, events, and dinners: "So, what do you do?" Many of us cringe when asked about our profile, and writing our own bio is challenging even for professional writers. Not because we don't really know, it's just a lot, or maybe feeling like too little, depending on where you are in your career. Searching for relevant experiences and stories, it's easy to drown among the alternatives. Or maybe you are in a transition, like my client who had made the bold step of leaving a high position in the corporate world to start her own coaching business. "It's the moment I meet new people, how do I tell the story about my company, and what do I write on my website?" Here's the process I created for her.

Starting out, take a look around and see what kind of bios and career stories that you like. In addition to website sections with *About Us*, streaming through the profile text on some of your LinkedIn contacts can give you a sense of different approaches. If you are a business owner, you want to make sure that the benefits for the customer are clearly stated. By using a personal story with something from your early years that's connected to your profession, you are drawing them in, showing why you are the one to choose among other providers. It's great to have a sense of different styles and the tone of voice you would like to come across with before you get going. For the questions below, use the creative writing guidelines and write five minutes for each question. If you have more to say when the minutes are done, just add on as it comes.

For recruitment at one of the most visionary government agencies in Dubai:
If you had a superpower, what would it be?
Which movie star is most like you?
If you could ask us (your company or client) a question, what would it be?
What is your biggest failure?

From a global consulting company:
What do you believe have been the most valuable life experiences you've had that shaped the person you are today?
How do you think this relates to your desire to explore a career move?
What are you deeply passionate about? How does that relate to your desire to work as X?
Is there anything else that you'd like to share with us?

Bio template from a European training company I worked with:

I went into X because:

- *I've always welcomed and liked changes, challenges, and growth. I worked…*
- *I am always X.*
- *My mission and passion is…*

My participants—clients—colleagues appreciate me for:

- *My* ____________________
- *My* ____________________

I get work satisfaction most from…

- *My* ____________________
- *My* ____________________

If you would like to use a more classic pitching format, this basic structure of a core idea sheet can be applied for projects, business ideas, and yourself as a business resource:

Problem or opportunity ____________________

Idea ____________________

Which will

1. ____________________
2. ____________________
3. ____________________

And to do that I need ____________________

When you have the drafts, type them into your laptop. You might want to keep a couple of versions to be used in different contexts.

Now comes the time to choose among the texts you have produced, and edit, edit, edit. It's a good idea to take a break and do something else to shift space between writing and editing. In the best-case scenario, have a night's sleep, or listen to a song, do the dishes, make a call. This gives you fresh eyes when you look at the text again from an editing perspective. The end result should be short, preferably no more than 250 words. Getting there will take some rounds. Once you have a version you like, share it with someone you trust. And if you feel comfortable, try it on a customer or someone you don't know that well—sometimes the best feedback comes from strangers. Don't be too perfectionistic, it's better to start using a first version right away. A bio is a living document, and it's sure to be tweaked again and again as you evolve and have new things to add as well as new insights about how to make it alive. When you have it ready, even standing in line at the supermarket can be an opportunity to make connections and find new clients or job opportunities.

Diary in a Flash

Another way to get going with your writing is keeping a journal. Something happens when we find the words and get them down on paper. Reading through what you wrote, you'll see your current state from the outside, helping you process emotions and questions. And while you are at it, you are practicing your self-expression and storytelling ability. If it feels overwhelming to write down your thoughts and it's like your pen just can't move fast enough, here's a method that might be easier for you to try. Start by placing the date in the middle of the page, maybe with a short comment below, for example, "sleepless" or "after dinner with Julie," and then draw some lines in different directions from the date. Beside the end of each line, add a few words describing what is going on for you, for example, "morning meeting with Siri, was she disappointed?"

"physical drain, check yoga center," "dropping project, relief." To get your emotional state down on the page in a blink, you can use a couple of symbols that make it easy and fast to show what you're feeling, like bubbles for gratitude or well-being, and a bolt of lightning zigzag for pain or sadness. This mind-mapping concept allows you to instantly zoom in and out of your situation. Flicking back through the pages, you get an emotional imprint of yourself at a certain time, without the need to read a text as such. I personally use both versions depending on the mood. Sometimes I find it helpful to process with full sentences, and when I want a quick download, I choose the visual one.

Chapter Six

Strategize Right

Getting Your Message Through

Strategize Right

Getting Your Message Through

The most important things in life are the connections you make with others.

—Tom Ford

The obstacles we come across when trying to reach others come in many shapes and forms. It can be a relationship, the "all eyes on me" moment, or the daunting phase of establishing new clients. In this chapter you'll find a collection of different communication tools, most of them created on the spot during an individual session. By asking the client to think about a high-stake situation where it's really important to get the message through or a context that is challenging, various topics emerge, and with them, different solutions. Here they are for you.

Power Structures and Layers

The head of talent management in a global engineering company was struggling with her boss. Needing to step up with a more assertive approach to grab the attention, we were deconstructing some sample interactions. When faced with a roadblock like this, it's helpful to go deeper and explore the underlying layers of what is going on. Starting out, we looked at how the power structure was affecting both of them. Often forgotten in communication training, this aspect trumps the others, whatever the circumstances. One of my favorite examples demonstrating this comes from a participant in the advertising industry who was presenting a new commercial, together with his creative team, to their CEO. They had worked hard to get it right, using humor as the attractor for their audience, and it ended up being hilarious. In this case, though, the CEO didn't speak the language in the movie, and so, while he was watching with a stone face, no one could move a muscle. Until the CEO had left, and they all collapsed, rolling on the floor laughing. For challenging interactions, reflecting through these layers can be helpful:

Power Structures—explicit—implicit—How do they play out?—What does the other person need to feel that his or her position is respected?—How can you express your concerns or input while connecting them to the strategic goals of the overall situation?

Roles—Expectations in this specific situation—Are they clear? Has something occurred that requires adjustments? Are you moving outside of your perceived role—if so, are you explaining your motives?

Communication Tools—What did you do?—Look at your behavior—body language—tone of voice—timing—emotional charge—materials, or examples you brought along to clarify your input.

Inner Dialogue and Spoken Words—Our presence is connected to the thoughts we are having. It can be useful to write them down in a column on a page, showing what was going on inside our head, and then add a second column with the words that we expressed during the challenging situation. Check if there are ways to minimize the difference between thoughts and spoken words. The more aligned, the more our inner dialogue will support the outcome we desire.

Words in Writing

During an intimate coaching group in a global trading company, one of the commercial directors brought the challenge of harsh emails going back and forth with a foreign client. Looking through the email stream from the last weeks, we discussed what could be done to improve the communication, and with that, the relationship between them. Here are my guidelines for email correspondence:

Are you listening in your reply? During one of my sessions with Active Listening, one of the participants asked if listening applies to writing as well. Indeed it does. Before you start your reply, have you read through the email you are answering? We all know how irritating it is to receive a reply showing that the person hasn't read what we wrote. The extra attention pays off in the rapport you are creating with your receiver.

Check your spelling. As one of my professors in business communication said, "When you are not there, your writing represents you." And you don't want your representative to show up with flaws that weaken your message. Edit an extra time, and read through before clicking send. Our flow of thoughts is faster than our fingers on the keyboard.

If uncomfortable, save it for a conversation. It's so easy to let off steam in an email reply, especially in situations of urgency. When you are triggered by an email, the best thing to do is wait. If possible until the next day, or at least, take a break and come back. We often misinterpret when we are irritated, and reading the email closely a second time might reveal something you hadn't noticed. If you still feel there are issues to be addressed, the best thing to do is to grab the phone and get on a call. If you are in the same building, try walking over to the other person and talk face to face. Emails are there to deliver messages, good news, and agree on next steps, not to share negative emotions. No matter how upset you might be, make sure the ending keeps the door open. It requires some discipline, but it's so worth it.

Think about your legacy. I once heard a story told by a woman who survived the concentration camps during World War II. Her family had been chased to the train station in haste, and being the big sister, she reprimanded her little brother for lingering to find his favorite toys. They were separated into different train wagons and she never saw him again. Living on with her words that could not be erased, her message was clear. Each time you deliver a message, make sure it would be all right if this is the last greeting you get to give.

Timing of the Message

"My boss just doesn't listen, he doesn't take me seriously!" Working as a reservation agent at an international hotel group, my client was eager to share her discoveries for new solutions. The frustration she felt talking about it made her eyes tear up. We started by looking at her delivery, shifting the focus from her manager's reaction to what *she* was doing.

Asking about her body position in a typical situation like this, I found out that she was seated at her desk when she had a new idea to share. The instructions for next time were to leave what she was doing and walk over to his desk, so she would be close when she started talking to him. Then I asked her about the timing, had she considered what would be a good moment for her manager to receive a new message? And what about the mode of communication—maybe it would be better to send him an email first with some bullet points about her discoveries, suggesting to speak with him the next day? When we met for our following session, a big smile was lighting up her face. She had done it all: sending an email first, followed by a conversation while being conscious about her body position. The result came straight away. "He is acknowledging my strengths, he said he can see that I am passionate about it." Looking back, she recognized that she had been impatient, sharing her thoughts the moment they arrived, not taking the time to be strategic and connect them with the agenda of her manager. Sometimes taking that one step back to reflect on how and when to deliver your message is all it takes.

The Wow Speaker and the Dialogue Speaker

My client was struggling with the "all eyes on me" moment. As a successful PR agency owner, part of her role was pitching the company to new clients on a regular basis. When we started our process, the evening before a new pitch would be flooded by nerves, getting more and more intense as the appointment came closer. In addition to her own struggle, she felt extra pressure by comparing herself to a colleague who would walk into any presentation while making it up on the fly. We named it "the wow speaker"—the personalities who simply take the space, able to talk about anything at any time. And yes, they can be impressive, lifting the room with exclamations and amazement. However, there are more ways to do it. While the wow speaker has charisma and masters many speaking tools, they sometimes have a tendency to feed their ego with the audience moment. It's both understandable and tempting. If we have the slightest need for approval or admiration, a group in front of us can be very seductive. Of course, in situations with big audiences and a setup that doesn't allow for interaction and questions, this approach is what is called for.

And then, there's "the dialogue speaker." These speakers leave their ego behind as they enter the room, giving the talk as an act of service. If possible, they use real questions from the audience, adjusting the content to the input they receive. To them, the needs of the moment are more important than whatever was rehearsed. For the business pitches my client was delivering to small groups of people with specific requirements, the dialogue speaker was the desired approach. Leaning toward it helped increase her confidence. She didn't need to wow them; it was fine to share her story as opposed to trying to impress. A few sessions later, she came back and shared how she had stopped herself in front of a client. Anchoring herself in his needs rather than her own agenda, she could sense that she lost his attention and asked him whether this was what he was looking for. When he said no, she simply wrapped up and suggested a new appointment with a revised content. If she had been stuck with doubts about herself as a speaker, she wouldn't have been able to make the switch.

Different contexts require different styles, and while the wow effect is great on stage, if you can, include some parts of the dialogue speaker when you enter. In my experience, this is the speaker the audience wants to hear again.

Numbers That Count

It was only a few days away from the yearly gala dinner for specially invited corporate partners, each giving a certain amount to the global nonprofit every year. These were the donors who pretty much made it possible for the organization to survive, and the entrance ticket alone was an investment. My client had chosen a black chiffon dress for the occasion. It was her voice that needed to convince over a hundred guests out there that their funding had a real value. Not only to the nonprofit but also to themselves and the companies they represented. She had done her homework, gathering relevant data and preparing the stories that would connect the dots. Our focus was the last bit, polishing her words to reach through the glamour and land the message in their hearts. The introduction was about human conditions drowning in the constant maelstrom of news stories, making us numb. Then came the data, half a million children without homes right next door. Stories about individual destinies, suffering, and solutions. All leading up to what the organization was doing. "This year, we reached 166 million children…" And this is where I paused her. Without an example to make it real, a number like this passes us by, leaving no trace of engagement behind. By presenting the number with a comparison that is close to the audience, you give them time to grasp what you have just said. In this case, relating it to the population of the donor's country of residence was impactful. "Ladies and gentlemen, take a moment to look at the UAE from above. We are around ten million people living here today. And now, imagine every single one of us inviting a child to dinner. Each of us would need to do this seventeen times to reach the number of destinies that our organization is touching with your help this year alone. Now…*that's* a lot of children." When she was done, the audience was showering my client in applause, and many came up with tears in their eyes and personal thank-you's. Her talk had hit home. Statistics and numbers can be a great asset in your presentation. When used correctly, they come alive, deepening the point you are trying to make.

Presence versus Control

We were preparing for a true high-stake presentation. My client was only a few weeks away from starting his new position as assistant director for an esteemed finance institution. On his first day in the new office, he was to introduce himself to the team. Around twenty-five people would be observing their new boss closely and he wanted to make the best of these first minutes. While preparing, we landed on one quality being more important than the others—showing everyone in the room that he cared. It might not sound that difficult, but part of the challenge for this client was a stiffness that overcame him when presenting. From being a charming and warm conversational partner, when he started practicing the contents of the speech, his face almost froze. After working on storylines, structure, and tone of voice, the piece that was missing was simply feeling confident enough to be fully present and let the moment unfold. For my client, who had a tendency to double-check details and almost over-prepare, this part wasn't easy. To be fully present, we need to give up control, and this requires trust. As a last step, I suggested an exercise that allows you to feel protected while resting in your comfort zone called the **Blue Light Exercise.** This is how you do it:

Place yourself in a relaxed position, sitting or standing, while connecting with your feet. Imagine fine roots growing out from below the soles of your feet toward the center of the earth, and feel how they keep you grounded. Now move your attention to the top point at the back of your head, and imagine a thin blue line coming down all the way from the sky, and connect with your head. This line holds you up, so you don't need to use any energy to keep seated or standing. Take three deep breaths, and feel the vast journey between the soles of your feet to the top of your head. Connect with the blue light in the line from above, and inhale it into your legs, your torso, your arms, and your head. As you feel your body filled up with light, start exhaling it out around you, so it becomes a sphere of blue light. Stretch out your arms, and let them sway from side to side, marking the boundary of your sphere. Let your arms fall, and take three breaths while relaxing. This is your protected space where you can feel safe and free to express yourself. Do the exercise the same day of your special moment, and take a deep breath before entering the room to reconnect with your blue light sphere. If you are one of those who have a hard time letting go, this exercise is for you.

Tips for First Encounters

How do we make the best of those networking moments? The energy was bouncing around the room between us as we explored the fine-tuning of every possible detail to make that first encounter an impact to last. As partners of a consulting group for the construction sector, my clients were exposed to a wide variety of settings, everything from casual to charged with tension. Starting out with the mammal level, I explained how the first moments serve to sniff each other out, while our senses are flooded with signals and impressions, pretty much like a couple of dogs with their tails wagging. This is one of the reasons it's so hard to remember a name after a few minutes of conversation. Firstly we are focusing on whether this is someone we can trust—far more important than a name. If you want to remember it, make sure you repeat it a few times, asking if you are pronouncing it correctly, if the name has a meaning, or where it's from. Here are more tools to leverage your networking moments.

Attitude Alignment

We tend to forget—encounters consist of ourselves as well as the other person. One of the components affecting how a conversation unfolds is the inner wavelength we are bringing. If you are telling yourself something along the lines of "I know these types, all pumped up and boring," it will color off in a very different way than for example "I wonder who these people are, we might have something in common." People are not absolutes, and our approach is part of making those remarkable connections possible.

Pause and Sense

When we walk into a room full of people, we have a tendency to rush into the first cluster of people we see, eager to join the buzz, especially if the others have started before we arrive. A different approach is to take a moment and sense where the energy is before you move on. By doing this, you are choosing which conversations you want to join. And if your moment of taking it all in lasts for a while, that's fine. Centering yourself can be a way to let people come to you.

Audience Awareness

Be mindful of who you are standing in front of, and try to find out something about his or her needs before launching into your personal pitch. If there's little interest in your services, try digging into what the other person is doing and see what comes up. I experienced the opposite during a speed networking session at a conference a while back, where my speaking partner tried to sell me a software solution with HR tools for big corporations. The fact that I had introduced myself as an independent trainer had no effect on what she said. Her concept of networking was to bring a preprogrammed pitch and repeat it to whoever came her way. If she would have listened to me when I explained my profile, she could have received some much-needed tips on how to get her message through instead!

Make It Personal

Engaging with new people, the most important thing is not to tell them what you do, but to create a connection. It can be anything: pets, exercising habits, how you cook your broccoli. Think about it. When you come home after an event or a working day in a big organization, who do you feel in impulse to help, a professional profile or a person? Of course, for someone to support us, they need to know what we are looking for. But the impulse to do so comes from having a sense of who we are.

Active Listening

Meeting someone who has the capacity to listen to us, really taking in what we are saying, is a rare luxury, especially in a speedy networking context. When it happens, time stops, and we get to feel how the whole is greater than the sum of its parts, making life bigger. A colleague recently posted a question on Facebook, asking what we do to win others over. "What is *your* way, what do you do to influence them?" My answer was simple. "Listen."

Passion Giveaways

The best way to meet new people is inviting them into your own passion space. It goes without saying, in this context you will be in your comfort zone and filled with energy. What better way to welcome new contacts into your life? If you are creating a network in a new city or targeting a new segment of the market, find a way to offer whatever you love doing for free. Starting out with this, you will generate contacts and goodwill, eventually leading to potential career growth. For me who loves the joy of singing, the first thing I did when arriving in San Francisco and

Dubai was starting a choir. In addition to giving me a safe space where I could recharge my batteries, I had a topic to introduce when meeting new people, inviting them to try out a rehearsal. The activity you engage with can be anything; the only criterion is that it's something you love giving away. A therapist I know started out in Peru by giving free tarot-card readings, and by the time her savings were up, she had enough credibility and word-of-mouth referrals to start charging. And a client of mine who wanted to break in as a personal trainer started by giving free golf lessons at a club, promoting both his own skill set and the club. Your passion for whatever it is that you love will help you find venues and people to share with.

Chapter Seven

Connect Right

Creating Rapport in My Career Cities

Connect Right

Creating Rapport in My Career Cities

Life begins at the end of your comfort zone.

—Neale Donald Walsch

With a freelance career like mine, moving from country to country undoubtedly pushes the bar up toward the sky. In some ways, it's really not a wise career decision. Yet shifting base and populations comes with matchless gifts. Living in other places, you acquire a fluidity and an ability to see things from different perspectives, questioning "the given." To me, the thrill of adding more nuances and aspects of the human condition makes it all worth it despite the humbling experience of starting from scratch.

As a communicator, this is the ultimate test. Learning how to bridge your learned ways with the unknown, it's unavoidable to make mistakes as you face challenges you couldn't even have imagined. And then suddenly one day, you start noticing how new insights have landed. While expanding your comfort zone, your new hometown has become a part of you. I am forever grateful to these cities and the people who let me make them mine. Each of them has sharpened my tools to connect through whatever comes my way.

This chapter is organized around Copenhagen, Barcelona, San Francisco, and Dubai, with some factors making it attractive to have them as your home base, a story about something I learned while working there and a couple of characteristics to consider before a potential move.

Working in Copenhagen

The first thing that comes to my mind when I think about Copenhagen and Denmark is the untranslatable word "lun." In the dictionary you find: warm snug, cozy, humorous. It's a special approach that only Danes know, like the way a bus driver welcomes you on board with a relaxed tone and friendly expression or the humor that comes across in Danish movie commercials, appealing to your humanness while making you smile inside. If you live there long enough to learn Danish and soak up the cultural codes, you'll get your share of "lun" encounters.

Work-Life Balance

The Scandinavian countries have a work-life balance you won't find anywhere else. It's not a coincidence or newly invented phenomenon. The fight for dignified working conditions started with workers organizing in unions already in the late 1800s. If you have the opportunity to visit while in town, I recommend a visit to *Arbejdermuseet*, the Workers' Museum, on Nørrebro. The building itself, with its ceremonial hall and cellar restaurant kept in original style, is amazing. And you'll see one of the original banners with 8-8-8, the worker's call for eight hours workday, eight hours free time, and eight hours sleep. Sadly relevant in today's working markets around the world. There's been research done about the efficiency when keeping workdays short, and it shows how it pays off for production and ROI. One of the senior executives in a multinational company that I worked with told me how his transfer to a Nordic country was an intentional decision to sustain his family life. This was the only location he could be a father and keep his position at the top. A once–in-a-lifetime opportunity to be found nowhere else.

Healthy Values

For those of you who are following the World Happiness Report, you already know that Denmark has hit number one again and again. Gallup provides the data for the report with various indexes such as GDP per capita, social support, healthy life expectancy, freedom to make life choices, generosity, and trust. With a strong civil society, a well-functioning democracy, and corruption down to almost zero, the foundation for critical thinking and new ideas is in place, and the country is a leading nation when it comes to sustainability, innovation, and urban planning. The best way to get your taste of the urban landscape is to rent a bicycle and follow the paths across canals and bridges while enjoying your own traffic lights for bicycles. And be prepared, finding a parking spot for your bike at a popular cinema or subway station can be just as hard as finding a spot for your car in other cities!

Early Learning

I was doing my first official job as a drama teacher at a folk high school on Amager. Another brainchild of Denmark, this educational concept was designed in the mid-1800s. Rather than focusing on diplomas and career results, these schools aim at developing interests and a dynamic mindset for men and women to be able citizens. When I got the contract, I was filled with a special knowing. This was my first career step. I celebrated by drinking a solemn cup of coffee at Bjørg's Café by the Town Hall Square. The adventure had begun. And an adventure it turned out to be. After a few sessions, my new boss called me in to her office for a check in, discreetly asking me to be mindful when I instructed. "It's important that everyone can participate, so please don't make it too physical, someone might feel left out. And oh, we want to make sure that no one feels sad during the sessions, so please don't upset them." I didn't know whether to laugh or cry. A drama class without movement and emotions is like writing a book without using too many words—pretty impossible. I continued with the sessions, learning as we moved along, and despite her concerns, it went well. And then one day, I made a classical beginner's mistake as a facilitator. Doing my very best to ensure that this would be valuable for the participants, I had used hours preparing the session, and the outline was a long list of exercises, each leading into the next one. As a beginner, I was sure that the indicator for a great session was for the list to be delivered and done—we needed to produce something. The instructions were fast paced, and after a while, one of the elderly participants, short of breath, asked for a break. "Really, a break? In the middle of it all?" I can still remember the sting of impatience in my body while I was looking for the right response. "OK, let's just do one more exercise and then we'll take a break." I am sure my old-time participants have forgiven me. Maybe they didn't even mind that much. To me, this is the scene I carry to remind me that the needs of the participants always come first. If one voice speaks up, it's representing several others in the room. Today I know better. A few years back I wrote an article, "Five Guidelines for the Master Trainer," and the second one goes: The younger we are as trainers, the more wedded we are to getting through our agendas, yes, we even think that this is the measure of success. And then, the more experience we gather, the more flexible we become as we learn that being present in the moment, being able to dive into the needs of the participants and do whatever is called for here and now, is the real art of any session.

Nordic Work Culture

Informality

Danes are known to be relaxed, often dressing down when you expect the opposite. Don't misinterpret the easygoing attitude with easy access to becoming one of them. It's a communication style and not an entrance ticket. When you are invited to a party, you might miss the regular introductions as you enter. It will often be a "Hi" as you open the door while you are expected to find your way into the mingling groups. And when you find yourself with a family or small gathering, you might feel awkward, missing the questions you would expect to the newcomer in the room. It's not bad intentions, just a matter for you to find a way to join the conversation when you have something to add. Most probably, the probing into who you are and where you are from will come when you are sitting alone with one of them.

Humbleness Required

One of the more subtle codes for social behavior that you'll notice when you start interacting with coworkers and friends is the Jante Law. The concept comes from the Danish-Norwegian author Aksel Sandemose, in his novel *En flygtning krydser sit spor* (A Fugitive Crosses His Tracks) from 1933. Sandemose criticized the narrow-minded mindset of a small town called Jante, where the inhabitants abide by these laws:

1. You're not to think *you* are anything special.
2. You're not to think *you* are as good as *we* are.
3. You're not to think *you* are smarter than *we* are.
4. You're not to convince yourself that *you* are better than *we* are.
5. You're not to think *you* know more than *we* do.
6. You're not to think *you* are more important than *we* are.

7. You're not to think *you* are good at anything.
8. You're not to laugh at *us*.
9. You're not to think anyone cares about *you*.
10. You're not to think *you* can teach *us* anything.

Also felt in the rest of Scandinavia, they can be boiled down to one sentiment: you are no better than anyone else. It's another shade of equality and community, the values that permeate the Danish culture. When you interact with others, don't try to impress. It's wise to be careful with superlatives about yourself and your country of origin. The best way to win people over is to be humble and sing the praise of Danish discoveries that you have encountered which, luckily, isn't difficult at all.

Working in Barcelona

Mentioning Barcelona makes people smile. It's a city that conquers the heart with its mixture of history and architectural beauty. Moving around town, there's eye candy in every direction. When I think of the city, I see the narrow streets of my old gothic neighborhood with metal shutters loudly rolling down to mark the lunch siesta and tiny shops cut into the stone walls with a mix of high-end design and fashion for grannies. And drinking *cortados*, a miniature latte with more coffee and less milk in the neatest little serving glass, the best coffee combination you can get.

Flowery Encounters

Talking to people in Spain is not like talking to people anywhere else. For someone from the North, it's almost frightening at first with the sudden explosions of increased volume when the intensity heightens. And the language, ah, the words, flowery and flattering, and *totalmente lleno de flores*. People are delighted and *encantado*s and full of adjectives.

You don't need to know someone that well. It's enough to have your first business lunch or coffee and out of nowhere you land in a wavelength of sharing from the heart, just like that. I had lived there quite a while when I suddenly realized, it's just like in the old Almodóvar movies, where the characters switch from being strangers to telling each other everything in a blink. And the one- to two-hour lunch breaks with three courses are perfectly designed to start off. In Barcelona, people know how to enjoy.

Innovative Catalonia

This northeastern corner of the Iberian Peninsula has been testing and experimenting for centuries, and to my knowledge, it's the most innovative part of Spain. Being a hub for innovation, you can feel the appetite to try new things in a society that embraces pioneers while respecting traditions and quality. It's no coincidence that I ended up working for Infonomia, the biggest innovation consulting firm in the Spanish-speaking world, and I was asked to develop a workshop with right-brain skills for a master's degree in innovative hospitality management. If you have the chance to visit Infonomia's yearly conference, the Business Imagination Fest, it's a vibrant place to soak up the newest tendencies of what's moving and shaking.

Golden Moments

Barcelona was a generous pathway on my career journey, turning into a wide boulevard of experiences. I was allowed to open the doorway to emotional intelligence for a group of technical architects in the medieval village of Vic. I helped the European Commission access their voices, and advertising agents shed tears over their stories as we entered presentation mastery. By the time my next career destination emerged, I needed a way to wrap up with gratitude. At the time I was leading an a cappella group with two other women, and my apartment on Carrer de Sant Pere Mitjà had a mesmerizing view of antennas and rooftops, with a staircase from the terrace leading up to the roof. Wanting to make the circle whole, I invited the participants who had been in my hands throughout my years in town for a mini concert under the stars. Looking out at the crowd standing around me, I could see the faces of the participants from my first humble workshop for a group of businesswomen, to politicians, students, medical doctors, and my favorite CEO of all times, inspiring Pilar, who combined philosophy and ethics into her leadership of engineers in risky environments. I wasn't prepared for the emotions that overcame me. These people had made it possible for me to advance from a newcomer to an authority in my field—I owed them so much. In my welcoming speech, I shared how many people had told me that the idea of establishing myself in town was not going to work, naming countless examples of talented expats who couldn't get through to the Catalan market and ended up leaving after a few months. During my first winter, it did seem like a bad idea, and I had many moments of doubt before the assignments started coming. And here I was, surrounded by diversity, appreciation, and friendly smiles covering the rooftop. After the last a cappella song, we all joined together in a melody, our voices bouncing off into the dusk air. On the way out, I had placed a bag with a tag saying *los momentos dorados* and a pile of notepaper next to it, and when we ended, I asked them to share their memories and write a few words about what they were taking away from our sessions. It was their golden moments that made me realize: my sessions go deeper than learning a new skill, they can be transformative. "I learned to be myself without fearing what others will say," "In your class I saw myself—and I liked what I saw. We learned to accept ourselves—making us better for each other," "Thank you for returning me to myself." It goes both ways. My participants help me, allowing me to live my purpose and be of service.

Mediterranean Work Culture

Slowing Down in Tempo

Coming from a Nordic work culture, one of the first things I noticed in Barcelona was the need to slow down in tempo. During my first summer in town, I was eagerly waiting for July to end, so I could get started with business. August, I soon came to know, is the main vacation month here, as the heat gets too intense to work in. The locals escape the city by going to their summer homes in the mountains or by the sea. And I bought a bike to discover my new surroundings. My surprise continued throughout that first year as fiesta after fiesta rolled out. There are saints to be celebrated, spring onions, or *calçots*, to be eaten, processions with magical kings to be seen, and each neighborhood has its own street festival with decorations, food, and fireworks. If one of these festive holidays falls in the middle of the week, people make it a *puente*, meaning "bridge," taking the days off leading up to the holiday or the days coming after, meaning that you'll have a slow-motion effect for business for most of the week.

Catalan Sensitivity

Barcelona is the capital of Catalonia, and the locals see themselves as Catalans, not Spanish. With a throwback to the oppression this region suffered during the Civil War and the Franco regime, it is understandable that feelings are stirred. It's not many generations ago since someone's family member was incarcerated for speaking Catalan, and there's been economic repression and tensions for decades. Be gentle with the way you refer to these matters when you interact with people. If you have the patience to learn Catalan, you'll create trust in a whole different way. A great way to deepen your references about the history of the city is by reading the novel *La Sombra del Viento* (The Shadow of the Wind) by Carlos Ruiz Zafón. The book takes you on a journey that is tightly connected to the streets and locations in town; you can even go on special tours with guides taking you to the sites of the book.

Working in San Francisco

It's almost impossible to get bored in the Bay Area. With an inexhaustible events calendar, it's one of the most exciting places to be. You can attend thought-provoking after-dark events at the scientific Exploratorium, learn about pitching at start-up gatherings, absorb mash-up choreographies by your favorite pop star with the Bay Area Flash Mob Group, and enjoy brilliant storytelling events in different formats. I delved into the solo-performance community, taking my first trembling solo steps at the Stage Werx Theatre, instructed by a fabulous stand-up comedian. No matter what you throw yourself into, you'll find the best of the best here. It's no coincidence that people flock from all around the world to get their taste of the magic.

Avant-Garde in Two Directions

Once arrived in San Francisco, you soon learn that you're in the middle of what is called "the Bay Area," containing the East Bay with Oakland and Berkeley, the North Bay with the Wine Country, the South Bay with Silicon Valley, and the Peninsula with San Francisco and other cities. This area is a unique combination of two streams of consciousness colliding in an unlikely fusion. On the one hand, it's a pioneer location for spirituality, New Age, and various kinds of therapies with a density of Buddhist centers and Eastern philosophy. On the other hand, it's a hub of innovation and entrepreneurship, with Silicon Valley attracting the cutting edge of tech development and start-ups. The two fields constantly feed each other with an influx of new concepts and excellence. Most likely, in whatever area you are working, you'll find trendsetters and like-minded people here, and what you'll end up doing when you get there might not even have been invented yet.

Curiosity and Engagement

The social wavelength is open and friendly, making it easy to meet new people. When you start sharing, you'll notice that they are genuinely curious and often supportive and resourceful when it comes to launching new ideas. Of all the places I have lived, I have never been invited so quickly to everything from dusk meditations to hiking trips and Christmas celebrations. As a newcomer, I also noticed a social engagement. Almost everyone I met was involved in some kind of volunteering, making the world a better place by contributing to their community. The drive to have a positive impact permeates the corporate sector as well. Tony Hsieh founded Zappos with a commitment to deliver happiness to both customers and employees in San Francisco, and on a much smaller scale, I gave an innovation workshop to Give Something Back in Oakland. As an office supplier, they use the social entrepreneurship model, engaging their customers by letting them choose which nonprofit organization they want to support with the yearly profit. The list of inspiring initiatives goes on, waiting for you to get involved.

Stardust and Presence

It was a larger-than-life moment. Driving toward Mountain View in Silicon Valley, my GPS was set for NASA Ames Research Center, where a group of audio engineers were waiting for me. We were going to have a session, sharing tips and insights about sound and voice. It had come about in the most organic way. A close friend knew the deputy division chief, who had showed me around the NASA premises beaming with enthusiasm and pride. I left with stories about rockets and launches, a folder with stickers and butterflies all over. I was going to come back to meet his team, this time invited as a voice expert. I felt like a follower being introduced to her favorite band. As a little girl, my father had sneaked me in to see the *Star Wars* movie before I had the proper age, and I had been a fan of planets and science fiction ever since.

Sitting in my car, a mix of gratitude and nerves was filling me up. This was the closest I could get to touch the stars of the sky—Milky Way here I come! But wait, what did I really know about the voice, would I have anything to add for these outstanding individuals, educated and fine-tuned in every way? And there, oops, an exit was missed, suddenly all senses focused in on traffic and roads. I couldn't be late, not for this one! My right hand was touching the documents ready to be handed over for my entry pass. By now the inner dialogue about my inferiority was the only thing I could hear. Even so, exits and entrances appeared, and I found myself walking into a room with a circle of chairs. When I had taken my seat and looked around, heads were turning toward me. In a few seconds, I would need to speak, this was my moment. I had to do something, I couldn't contribute feeling like this. That's when the word came from somewhere inside. "Presence." With a deep breath, I called on the rest of myself to arrive. I wasn't here to impress, the reason I was invited was to support these people with whatever I could. And to do that, the only thing I needed was to be right there. Once my focus shifted from me to the others in the room, I was able to listen. I soon found out, to some of the most interesting and dedicated people I had ever met and the session turned into simply having a great time among peers. When I came home that afternoon, I placed the NASA entry pass on my noticeboard. For months to come, it would remind me of the one and only gift we bring into any context. It's all about being present.

American Work Culture

Practice Self-Promotion

If you're not raised in America, it can be a rough ride to compete with a population that is born into a culture where pointing out your qualities is not only natural but required from an early age. A Swedish friend told me how she learned this during her time as a scenographer in New York. When she mentioned that she had done the design for Philip Glass' opera *Echnaton* and people were wowed, she'd respond with a comment about how the production was an amateur show, expecting people to probe for more details. Instead, they would lose interest and walk away. "You have to say how good it is and keep on with the superlatives, humility is out." Find ways to practice self-promotion unabashedly—you'll need the capacity to state your assets in both social and professional contexts.

Speaking Style

There's a lightness and sense of direction when you talk with people in America. Starting point and commonalities flow toward a solution of whatever matter is presented. In some situations it can be an advantage. If you have limited time and a problem to solve, nothing could be better. Coming from Europe, I noticed that something gets lost. It took me a while to pinpoint and then I realized. I am used to exploring a topic from different viewpoints, allowing for diverging tendencies that might not be an answer, but simply add to the depth of whatever is being discussed. One of my new San Francisco friends who had a European spouse gave me the words: "We're missing the art of conversation." An observation like this is generic, of course, and maybe not relevant for your context. If you find yourself longing for another way of sharing, it's good to know that it might be part of a cultural speaking code.

Working in Dubai

First thing to do when you arrive in Dubai is a drive down Sheikh Zayed Road, giving you that buzz of "everything is possible." The skyscrapers on each side crawl their way up toward infinity with glossy facades, and the metro stations look like right out of a science-fiction movie, indeed, most recently used in *Star Trek Beyond.* This is the city where everything glimmers and downtown is a fairy tale of blinking trees and dancing fountains.

I hadn't thought about it until my housemate from Copenhagen pointed it out during her visit. Decorations are everywhere, even a simple bridge is beautified with ornaments. Another friend who came to see my new hometown exclaimed, "It's like living in Tatooine from *Star Wars!*" Science-fiction fan or not, it's impossible not to feel the soaring conquest of the desert, triumphantly rising as a testimony of the undoable being done, eagerly inviting you to join the thrill.

Truly International

Wherever you go, the first two questions are: "Where are you from?" and "How long have you been here?" Dubai hosts around 200 nationalities living side by side, while the Emirati nationals make up as little as 10 percent of the population. In almost every context, you will find a mix of continents and traditions, erasing fixed standards and providing you with an abundance of perspectives. There's even a minister of tolerance to stimulate the coexistence of the diverse population. I've never been to a place with so many young and old Third Culture Kids, defined as children who grow up in another country than their parents. For these citizens of the world, languages are swopped daily and the sense of home has become a continuum. Transcending international, living here you become inter-belonging while making the world bigger.

Living the Future

The UAE was founded as recent as 1971, and the speed of development is mesmerizing. What is solid in other cities is in motion, like an organism growing out of its own shape, outdating maps and GPS routes in an explosive speed. Moving here, you become part of the future while you witness the city morphing into new buildings, parks, and canals. With an emerging market and an exceptional gap between undeveloped areas and opportunities, this is the Silicon Valley of the Middle East. Hosting the highest number of entrepreneurs in the Arab world, it's the dream destination for brave souls with big ideas.

What Do They Need?

It was just a remark while we were catching up on the phone about a coming assignment. The evaluations from last time weren't that great. Oh well, I thought, we knew that the group had been exhausted, and I had already shared with her how I redesigned the session on the spot to give the participants some extra time off. I didn't give it much thought until the next time we spoke. I had been an associate for her consulting company for over a year, and we enjoyed working together from the get-go, it couldn't be that bad. But this time her voice had a more serious tone. The company at the top of the food chain for this project was concerned about the feedback. I still didn't worry. As a typical Dubai assignment, in addition to my consulting colleague on the phone, there was yet another company between myself and the client, and they would never want to let me go either. And then the message came. I had been fired by the client on the top. It took a while for it to land. We had several workshops planned, and I had a string of excellent reviews behind me. A quick flashback took me to the time when I was about to start my career.

Wanting to save money, I had taken on a job as a waitress, and after two shifts, the manager let me go, giving me an extra push to get going with my workshops. But this was different. Throughout my years as a trainer, I had experienced a few flat sessions. But never had a long-term training client listened more to the evaluations than my take on the session.

Reflecting back, it started to make sense. For this group my style had been too direct, I needed to fine-tune my sensitivity. And then, of course, the obvious. The topic for my session had been presentation techniques and they didn't have any to work on at the time, alas, there was no need for what I was offering. As the fourth layer counting down from the deciding client, there was little I could do to ensure that my content was relevant to the receivers on the floor. As luck would have it, I had another session with the same topic a few weeks later. This time, the client was a prestigious mega-event organization, hosting a graduate program with a similar participant profile. Slightly shaken from my recent blow, I went in with low expectations. But my concerns were unnecessary. With their pitches coming up, my toolbox unfolded with a sparkly presence among the circle of heads around me, and by the time we came to the break, everyone was leaning in while the questions kept popping. When I describe what it feels like to my business coach, I say that it's like cutting chocolate cake, effortless and alive. Whatever we bring to the table, if our message isn't related to the people in the room, it won't fly. It's the match with their needs that takes you from fired to cake cutting.

Middle Eastern Work Culture—Dubai

Hellos and Goodbyes

Landing in Dubai, it's easy to meet people. Most of them have arrived at some point, going through the challenges of starting out, and they are eager to share from their experience and help you out. Once you have made it your home base, you start noticing that many of the contacts are temporary. In Dubai, people travel constantly, some for business and vacations and everyone for visits to their home countries. This is a place of sudden changes. If you lose your job, there's only a short window of time to find a new one before you need to leave the country, and every new season start after the summer, there's an influx of new Dubaians arriving while others are leaving the city behind. This makes up a transient social scene with a constant string of farewells. You'll need an elastic heart ready to open and close.

Decisions Take Time

When I arrived and one after the other told me that you need patience to make business in the UAE, I didn't really take it in. Carried high on the "I'm gonna make it here" vibe, I was sure this wouldn't apply to me. I soon started learning how very true their advice had been. I also learned that negotiating here is hardcore. If you're coming from Europe or the United States, chances are you'll find the approach aggressive, requiring practice and thick skin. And while the mix of multicultures is everywhere, it's crucial to learn about the Emirati culture with respect for etiquette and VIP structures, all coming down to that very needed patience.

Afterword

I consider myself privileged to have a comfort zone that spans over three continents. For my mother, Sissel, residing in our birth town Oslo, it can be quite a ride to follow the twists and turns as she hears updates from far away. When she sees photos from my latest endeavors, she will often say something about the unfamiliar surroundings followed by a surprised "And yet, in the middle of it all, I can see that you are totally yourself!" Recognizing my way of being me across whatever geographical distance between us has a soothing effect on her worry muscle. If I am genuinely present, it can't be that bad. And she's right. Finding a way to land with your whole self is both a pathway to well-being as well as a door opener to the connections you need to thrive. A few weeks ago, I met a new client who was looking for exactly this, finding her way to stay confident and responsive when interacting with others. As a young professional in a multinational company, she felt shy and slightly intimidated by the new co-workers she wanted to bond with. What was the secret to being more loose and relaxed? What could she do to connect with people on all levels of the hierarchy? While exploring her situation, I reflected through my toolbox. What would enable her to show up with the charming self she was sharing with me? Starting with the comfort zone, I reminded her that she was relaxed as we were talking, so no need to go out and look for comfort in other places. All that was needed was a way to bring it with her into more situations. I recommended self-acceptance, finding ways to be kind to herself, adding the *Breath of the Bull* to increase her body presence. Meeting with people of higher rank, it can often pay off to be the first one out to share something real about our self, giving the other person a chance to get a sense of us. If it resonates, he or she might follow with a comment or a question. And bringing curiosity makes it easier—if you really want to know what life is like in their shoes, the difference in position become less important. My young protégé came back in a whole new state. She had put the tools to use, and a common interest in a charity event had allowed her to connect with a challenging manager in a new way. In Denmark, they call it *det fælles tredje*, "the third in common," referring to the space that opens up when we engage in something outside ourselves and our roles, creating a space where we are equals. For my client, one session was enough to access her Right Kind of Loud.

My intention with this book is to pave the way for you to be confident, allowing you to offer the unique fingerprint of your personality and feel good with what is. All communication starts right there. Among the tools that I have shared, I hope you pick the ones you need as you move through your relationships and encounters. In case useful, here's a summary of the chapters:

1. ***Sound Right***—If you have a negative impulse when you think about your voice, you are not alone. Most adults feel some kind of discomfort around the way they are using it because of the restraining voice ideals that we grow up with and because the voice is so intimately connected to who we are. There's a lot to be gained by experimenting with it, both for yourself as a communicator and for your listeners.

2. ***Move Right***—The biggest hindrance for us to become more efficient with our body language is our tendency to stay up in our head with an overly mental focus. The gut brain is faster and receives and

sends more data than our mental brain. By connecting with it, we increase our charisma while tapping into nonverbal wisdom for decisions and deepened communication.

3. ***Listen Right***—We are usually not aware of how little we retain when we interact with others. Listening is far from passive, requiring both dedication and patience. At the same time, listening is the number-one skill when it comes to our ability to influence.

4. ***Speak Right***—Becoming a great speaker is not about trying to be as good as someone else. It's about finding the confidence for you to speak *your* way. Once you're there, it's all about leaving yourself behind and being present for the audience. In a funny way, the less you think about yourself and the more you think about *them*, the better you will be.

5. ***Tell It Right***—Writing is more than completing a task without making mistakes. It can be a door opener to stories and truths you didn't know you were carrying inside. When you write for yourself, you are healing your body, literally, while developing your writing voice.

6. ***Strategize Right***—Adding to the speaking and writing toolbox, this chapter also offers support for the framing and planning of your messages and for networking.

7. ***Connect Right***—High points and considerations to keep in mind before relocating to different work cultures. Plus learnings from my sessions, the importance of being responsive to the people you are interacting with, calling on your listening power in high-stake situations, and making sure your message is rooted in the needs of your audience.

During the writing process, I noticed how friends and clients started using the Right Kind of Loud as a way to refer to different situations. One of my test readers in California pointed out how the political discourse around him definitely wasn't the Right Kind of Loud. At a conference where I was the MC, I overheard visitors talk about how some speakers had hit the Right Kind of Loud, while others had missed out with a content that wasn't really adjusted to the audience in the room. And while describing a challenging negotiation to a friend, she spontaneously jumped in. "Ah, that wasn't the Right Kind of Loud, now was it…"

Using the Right Kind of Loud as a reference can be a segue to initiate conversations about a difficult situation at work, opening up for different points of view, or a gentle starting point to give feedback about something you need to address. Having worked with communication challenges in countless companies, I know how important it is to have a common language to cross the distance of misunderstandings and ambiguous messages, both among team members and while interacting with external stakeholders. We are already a community using the Right Kind of Loud to touch the hearts of our listeners, to retrieve our self-esteem after struggles and setbacks, to strengthen our branding voice, to break through the glass ceiling, to reach investors, and to increase our circle of influence. I would love for you to join us. With *the Right Kind of Loud*, there's no limit to our impact in the world.

Acknowledgments

Since I started writing, I have been showered with a wave of support that exceeded anything I could have imagined. Starting out, the title itself was a stroke of genius by fellow consultant Antoine Honoré while I asked for his input over lunch in Business Bay. He astutely observed my enthusiastic talking stream as being loud, and one, two, three, *the Right Kind of Loud* was born. A generous neighbor spent a great number of evenings listening to my first stumbling editing round, and when the time came to look for test readers, they kept volunteering from all sides. Some of them were people I ran into for the first time, insisting on supporting my process. An ex-client offered to introduce me to her fellow MBA students at Hult International Business School, providing me with the neutrality of test readers who'd never met me before. A colleague checked the energy level of the manuscript, while a friend put up with last-minute listening with our heads covered in highlighting foil at the hair salon. Another friend emerged with language advice for the appendices. And when I was standing in a horrendously long line to the check-in counter at Gatwick Airport, and the small talk with the backpacker in front of me revealed that he was a professional editor on his way to Hollywood, I used the opportunity to show him the table of contents and got it back with spot-on corrections that no one else had seen.

Heartfelt thank you to Afsheen Ismail, Anders Wickström, Arun C. Mandyan, Cecilia C. Braidy, Deborah Dowling, Disha Jana, Hayat Faysal, Jaffar Mahmoud, Jeff Crerie, Joe Ekker, Kathy Hrastar, Laura Toma,

Matus Horniacek, Miroslava Vavrova, Mohammad Al Jasmi, Samie Al-Achrafi, Sneha Joshi, and Sarfaraz Dawoodi.

I also extend my gratitude to Stress Expert Henrik Krogh for teaching me the Breath of the Bull and to Professor Michael J. Capek at Stern School of Business, New York University, for sharing the Active Listening method with me. Without your friendships my life would be so much poorer and my participants and book readers would be missing out big time. Another cornerstone for this book to be completed has been the unwavering support from my business coach Steve Hamilton-Clark, gotta love it! Julie Cottineau from BrandTwist pushed me to find crisp expressions and Brand School faculty member Alison Sheehy was a great resource for the book cover. My dear friend and the best photographer I've come across, Lisbeth Hjort did her magic with my portrait. Special thanks also to Mick Todd from 2bLimitless for exposing me to inspiring clients in Dubai.

Last but not least, my thanks goes to *you*. Like I said in the chapter about listening, this book is not communicating anything by itself. As a title in the bookshelf or a potential item in a shopping cart on Amazon, it remains a pile of random intentions. It is your reading process and making sense of the text that transforms it into meaning. I'd love to hear about your discoveries and successes with *the Right Kind of Loud*. You can find me on LinkedIn, Facebook, and Instagram. And you can always email me at **kimapage@kimapage.com**.

Appendix A
Overview of Exercises

1. Sound Right
Unleashing the Power of Your Voice

2. Move Right
Glowing with Your Presence

3. Listen Right
Winning People Over

4. Speak Right
Engaging Your Audience

Appendix B
Expression Glossary

The Right Kind of Loud—*fine-tuned communication approach that reaches your audience*

1. Sound Right

Unleashing the Power of Your Voice

- Full-body voice—*a voice that comes from the stomach, as opposed to a voice that comes from the throat or the head—p9*
- Voiceaholic—*addicted to exploring the voice—p12*
- Vocal wound—*a low self-esteem around the voice, caused by a painful and often embarrassing experience in childhood or youth—p15*
- Vocal inhibition—*hindrance to using the voice effectively—p17*
- Voice elasticity—*the ability to modulate the voice—p24*

2. Move Right

Glowing with Your Presence

- The gut brain (the stomach brain)—*an autonomous nervous system inside our intestines—p30*
- Breath of the bull—*slow-motion breathing exercise—p32*
- High and low status signals—*body language signals showing dominant or submissive positions—p37*
- The status swinger—*the ability to adjust your status signals—p40*
- Micro expression—*facial expressions moving in very high speed, showing the real feeling of a person—p43*

3. Listen Right

Winning People Over

- Concentration muscle—*the ability to concentrate—p48*
- Cleansing your gaze—*seeing your surroundings with an open mind—p51*
- Attention muscle—*the ability to stay attentive—p58*

4. Speak Right

Engaging Your Audience

- The prayer of the audience—*the wish inside an audience member for the talk to be special—p60*
- The contract between the speaker and the audience—*the agreements of behavior during a presentation—p62*
- Sacred pauses—*pauses that increase audience connection—p62*
- Audience ally—*someone you trust to give you feedback after your talk—p68*
- Bathing in yourself—*an exercise where you focus on feeling good about yourself—p71*

5. Tell It Right

Writing Your Story

- Show, don't tell—*enable the reader to experience the story as opposed to being told what is happening (Originally coined by playwright Anton Chekhov)—p82*
- Word wonder—*interest in the sounds and meanings of words—p83*

6. Strategize Right

Getting Your Message Through

- The wow speaker and the dialogue speaker—*different approaches when it comes to relating to the audience—p96*
- The blue light exercise—*helping you feel safe when you're nervous—p99*
- Attitude alignment—*becoming aware of your thoughts and judgments when you meet new people—p101*

7. Connect Right

Creating Rapport in My Career Cities

- Inter-belonging—*belonging to more than one country—p119*

Afterword

- The worry muscle—*the tendency to worry—p123*
- Det fælles tredje (the third in common)—*a common field of interest between two speaking partners—p124*

About the Author

Kim A. Page is a passionate trainer and speaker with an embodied approach, helping clients get their message through, using their voice and body language, influencing people with active listening, and giving unforgettable presentations. She has supported leaders and team members in multinational and local organizations as well as nonprofits such as Emirates Palace, the European Commission, NASA, Greenpeace, Volkswagen, and Abbott.

With a background as a singer and performing artist, she learned how to hone a message and create audience connection on stage, and she has directed choirs and shows with a wide variety of participants. After years of training in various voice techniques, Kim developed a methodology to address vocal inhibitions and help clients access the full potential of their voice as a communication tool. As a vocal coach, Kim has worked with all kinds of professionals, spanning from politicians to engineers and CEO's, and she has led the corporate Choir of Atkins, Dubai for employee wellness.

Kim received her bachelor's degree in dramaturgy—the study of how to shape a story so it touches the audience, from Lund University, Sweden, and her master's degree in organization development from Sonoma State University in California. As a faculty member and guest lecturer, she has contributed at universities such as Carnegie Mellon University, Copenhagen Business School, Universitat de Barcelona, and Haas School of Business, UC Berkeley. She has had several articles published about communication competencies, and she is fluent in six languages.

Kim has fine-tuned her toolbox and ability to serve the needs of the moment throughout twenty years as a facilitator and speaker with a career that stretches across three continents, from Copenhagen, to Barcelona and San Francisco, before landing in Dubai, where she currently resides. She invites readers to email her at **kimapage@kimapage.com** and to visit her website at **www.kimapage.com**.